Lower East Side

ORAL HISTORIES

Lower East Side

ORAL HISTORIES

INTERVIEWS BY NINA HOWES

Edited by Eric Ferrara

THE
History
PRESS

Published by The History Press
Charleston, SC 29403
www.historypress.net

Copyright © 2012 by Eric Ferrara and Nina Howes
All rights reserved

First published 2012

ISBN 978.1.60949.794.1

Library of Congress CIP data applied for.

This book is dedicated to the generations of people whose dreams, sacrifices and creativity have made the Lower East Side such a unique and wonderful soul brew.

Contents

CONTENTS

Acknowledgements

We would like to thank the following people: Terry Gregory at Educational Alliance, Sirovitch Senior Center; Morgan Jenness, formerly at New York Theatre Workshop; Carlos Jerome at Around the Block; Elizabeth Ruf at Theater for the New City; Jeana Musacchio at Cabrini Center for Nursing & Rehabilitation; Alex Roe at Metropolitan Playhouse; Angie Salgado at Lillian Wald Senior Center; Fern Schwartz at Educational Alliance, Whittaker Senior Center; Hanya Krill at the Ukranian Museum; and all the participants who shared their life stories.

Children cooling off at a fire hydrant in August 1943. *Courtesy of the Library of Congress.*

Introduction

This project was born in the summer of 2000, during New York Theatre Workshop's Community Day. Morgan Jenness, the associate artistic director, spoke about the importance of oral histories in bringing history to life. And I thought, "Yes! This is for me." A few months later, I saw a huge construction crane cutting the sky at Tenth Street and Second Avenue. I had never seen a crane on the Lower East Side before. I knew I had to act fast.

The neighborhood as I had known it was changing. I had to get stories before they were gone. At first I started with friends and friends of friends. Then I started going into stores and community centers. I interviewed over sixty people from various backgrounds: Puerto Rican, Ukrainian, Polish, Austrian, German, Italian, Indian, Chinese and African American. The stories spanned the time from the 1920s through the 1970s. They were edited for clarity, but each person's unique voice was left intact.

Each story is distinct. Even people who lived on the same block had different perceptions, but most everyone agreed they wouldn't trade growing up on the Lower East Side for anything—even with the hardships. And we're talking about the days when if you wanted a bath, you had to go to the public baths and pay a nickel. There was no central heating; you had to get coal or find wood for the stove.

Soon the streets became alive for me. I began to see the horses and pushcarts crowding on Houston Street, the boys playing stickball, the women rushing to work in factory lofts on Broadway. And by the East River, I could see the docks busy with ships and cargo and kids trying to steal a piece of coal when the guard wasn't looking. I could hear the congas pounding through the thick summer air and feel the steam of the water hydrants splashing on the tar streets. But more than these images, and what I loved most, was meeting people whose spunk, diversity and perseverance made the Lower East Side a soul brew.

While looking for a publisher, I had the fortune of meeting Eric Ferrara. Both sides of his family lived in the neighborhood for over a century, and his work in the community—as an author and with the Lower East Side History Project—made him appreciate the value of these interviews. His experience helped shape the project.

I've been around the Lower East Side for over forty years. In 2007, I was evicted from my charming but funky walk-up apartment where I lived for twenty years. The building was sold for $4.5 million to a real estate developer who lived in Europe. None of us had proper leases. I tried to rally my fellow tenants to action, but despite my efforts, we were put out. After that, the interviews took on a new meaning. I couldn't wait to get to them.

They made me remember the Lower East Side as I had known it. They made me smile and sometimes cry. They helped me to learn how people talk, how people remember and how people survive.

—Nina Howes

FRANKIE ALEXANDER

*Interviewed in February 2001 at a coffee shop at
Nineteenth Street and First Avenue*

I was born in 1951 and named Frank Alexander Martinez. As an actor, I had difficulty getting cast because they thought I was Puerto Rican, and I don't look Puerto Rican. So I dropped my last name. My parents...my father's from Peru and my mother's from Cuba...they originally came to this country for a better life just as a lot of other immigrants did.

When I was little, my father worked at a diner...in the kitchen, the grill...and washed the dishes. My mother was a housewife. My parents lived on the Lower East Side. We moved around quite a bit. I remember Sheriff Street. I was always looking out the window 'cause we were directly across the street from the Williamsburg Bridge. It was the subways going by, and the cars. And there was also a walkway for pedestrians. I remember those sounds. For some reason, it didn't affect me. So I'd always be looking at people going by in the cars, in the trains.

It was predominantly a Jewish neighborhood. My apartment was a walk-up on the fifth floor. It was a big haul going up and down those steps. In the summertime, we didn't have air conditioning or a fan either. How we survived those hot and humid summers, I can't imagine.

We didn't have extra money for shopping, but my mother would take me to Klein's on Fourteenth Street because of the air conditioning. It was nice and cool in there. My father, he liked rock and roll, doo-wop and stuff. Listened to it on his portable radio. Once we saw these teenagers in the hall. They were smoking, and my mother was afraid—this was the time of street gangs—and all of a sudden they started harmonizing. They were doing doo-wop right in the hall. It was because of the echo. And I remember my mother applauding, and they bowed. And some of them had the pompadours—the hair up and slick. Like the Elvis Presley look.

In the summertime, the kids used to open up the hydrants, and they used to cut out the cans. And there were a lot of beer cans. Rheingold was the top beer; it had a red label. And they had a Miss Rheingold. They'd open up the cans, both ends, and put it in front of the running water. They'd hold on to it, and it was like a hose. They used to spray it all over.

I remember my mother; she used to do our wash in the sink with a scrubbing board. And my father set up this clothesline from the back of our building to another building across the way. Everybody would hang their clothes out on the line. It was great in the summertime. In the winter it was something else. One time my mother pulled in the clothes and my jeans were stiff; they were frozen.

Later on, that building was being knocked down, so we had to move. We went to East Ninth Street between First and Avenue A. There were no trees at all on that block. You wanted trees, you go to the park. The reason we got that apartment was because my father was going to be the super. He was getting rent free, and he was getting twenty-five bucks a week. Plus he had his baker job, so he was ecstatic.

And I had two places to play: the streets and a backyard. It was more like an open space. It wasn't divided like they are now. And across the way, there was a good friend of mine, Butch. He was a fox terrier. I always wanted a dog, but my parents said no, so I became friendly with the people across the yard. It was an older couple, Mr. and Mrs. Ryan, Irish people. And they'd let Butch come out, and we'd play ball and chase each other.

I wanted Butch to be like Petey in the *Rascals*. And I wanted to have my gang. We had our own secret language, and we'd trade comic books. We wanted to have a barbecue in the backyard. And there were these old bricks, and I took them and I built a fireplace. And I got the screen that you have in refrigerators and put that on top.

I became friends with all the kids on the block. They were mostly Polish and Ukrainian. I think I was the only Spanish kid. We used to play a game called Scully. Now Scully, you need bottle caps for; it was on the street. We'd take chalk and draw thirteen boxes. If you struck the other kid's bottle cap, then you'd win that bottle cap. And we'd shoot with our fingers. As you got more experienced, you'd pick and choose your bottle caps. The best bottle caps were the ones with less indentations. This way you could control it.

Frankie Alexander on East Ninth Street in 2012. *Courtesy of Eric Ferrara.*

Another trick that I learned was getting crayons and melting the crayon inside the bottle cap to make it heavier. Yeah.

We also played stoop ball. We had Spaulding, and we had Pensy Pinkies. And we used to hit it off the stoop and according to the bounces…one bounce would be first base, two bounces would be second base, third base was a home run.

We'd play a game called Ring-O-Levio, which was more or less like hide-and-seek. Another New York thing: we'd take our skates—when they were falling apart—and make boxcars. We'd take a milk box, which was made out of wood in those days, and a two-by-four. And take two wheels from one end of the skate and two wheels from the other. And we'd have races. I used to take Butch and put him inside. He was cool. He went in there.

And then there was "Johnny on the Pony," oh man! There's one guy, and his back is up against the wall, and everybody else is bent over in a big chain. The other team would run and jump on our backs to try to break that chain. The worse was having a fat kid jump on your back; that was bad news.

We played street hockey. We'd grab a stick—not a hockey stick, just a stick—and hit the ball from sewer to sewer. I used to fall a lot; everyone's knees were banged up, but we still played. We did all kinds of crazy things. There was a candy store we'd go to on Ninth Street, between First and Avenue A. The owner, his name was "Deaf Guy." That's what we called him. In the back they had a big room, and he lived there with his wife and his son. He had hooked up a cord going from the door to the back of the store, and when somebody walked in, a bell would ring. We'd try to get in there and steal some candy, but he'd run right up.

And there was this big woman who lived on the first floor, and she'd always be looking out the window. She was the neighborhood gossip. And she had these big bosoms. And she had two pillows she'd rest on. She used to ask me to buy her the papers; there were a lot of newspapers out there—the *Herald Tribune*, *New York Post*, *Journal American*, the *World Telegram*. And how could I forget the *Daily News*, *New York Times* and *Village Voice*? And she'd give me the comics, so I got a cut out of the deal.

In the early '60s, there were a lot of beatniks moving into the neighborhood. The Lower East Side was where Bob Dylan and Alan Ginsberg were. The Fillmore East was a theater at that time; they had plays and poetry readings. There was one winter in '62, it snowed and we had fourteen inches. The schools were closed. We loved it.

I remember the older kids came over, and they were throwing powerful snowballs. We were trying to hit 'em back. And then they stopped; they just stopped. They were staring at the beatniks. This woman was taking off her jacket. She was unbuttoning her sweater. She was taking off her clothes in the middle of winter. The snowballs were melting in our hands. She was totally naked. And she ran across the street, and we were like…in shock. It was a fun time growing up there on East Ninth Street.

On Avenue A, there was a drugstore right on the corner of Ninth and Avenue A, and next door to that there was a luncheonette that had booths and had a soda fountain. I would go in there for milkshakes, cherry cokes and egg creams. I got introduced to egg creams by one of the kids on the block when I first moved to East Ninth Street. "What the hell is an egg cream?" I thought there was an egg in there. But there was no egg. There was chocolate syrup, a little bit of milk and seltzer. "Wow man, this is good!"

I remember the First Avenue Market, which now is Theatre for the New City. It reminds me of the Essex Street Market, which my mother used to go to when we lived on Sherriff Street. I remember pickle stores with big barrels of pickles, all down Essex Street. And the guy used to put his hairy arm in there and pick out a pickle. Pickles were two cents apiece. The First Avenue Market was an open market like Essex Street. They would have their spaces, their stalls—vegetables and stuff.

There was one place that I loved to go to 'cause it was all dairy. They had cheese; they had eggs galore—brown eggs, extra large eggs, jumbo eggs, small eggs, mini eggs, eggs from chickens, eggs from hens. And they had cheeses, all kinds of cheeses. It was right on Ninth Street between First and Second Avenue.

We used to get the eggs there, the cheese there. And right next door to that was a Ukrainian bakery. And they had a bread called Babka. And around the corner, right on First Avenue between St. Marks and Ninth Street, a friend of mine from Mary Help of Christians…his parents owned a fish store. They really had fresh fish. There were some fish that were swimming around 'cause they had a pool. They would have striped bass. It would be really fresh. It would be alive. It would be shaking. His father would hold it down and *bop!* Chop the head right off and gut it and filet it and pull out the guts.

Another kid, his father owned a pizza shop. The pizza was ten cents a slice. The Sicilian slices were fifteen. The soda was five cents. With a quarter, I could have a slice and a coke and have ten cents left over. And I'd play the jukebox…the Beatles.

Pierogies, yes! I remember tasting them, and I said, "Wow, this is good stuff!" They made pierogies with a wheat grain, kasha. And my mother

A fish merchant on First Avenue in 1943. *Courtesy of the Library of Congress.*

didn't like kasha, but she made it with meat. My mother…she'd come to get me. And the other kids' mothers…she'd be cooking pierogies, and they'd exchange recipes. Which was a nice change because my mother, being Cuban, all she would make was rice and beans.

And of course we had the Italians. My friend Charles on Ninth Street between Second and Third…his mother taught my mother how to bake pasta. One time a week I had "Italian," which was macaroni with sauce and cheese. I loved it. And then I had pierogies. And how could I forget the kielbasa! And it was a fun time. We were the Little Rascals. I came back to the block about six months after we moved to Coney Island. I missed the gang. I missed the fun. I missed Butch. I missed Deaf Guy. And I missed Tompkins Square Park. I missed all my friends. I wanted to come back to make sure my name was still there 'cause I carved it into the asphalt.

George Boyd

Interviewed in September 2003 at Theater for the New City,
First Avenue and East Tenth Street

I was born in New York City, in New York Hospital on York Avenue and Sixty-eighth Street. I was living in Harlem at the time. I lived there for about ten years. And then my family came to the Lower East Side. I'm not sure why. I had a couple of uncles who lived down here, so they said, "Why don't you move to the Lower East Side?" And we did.

My mother's from Tennessee—Nashville. She had a brother who was here, and he told her it was a better place to be. My father's from New York. They met up here. My father did maintenance work for the federal government. My mother was a homemaker until I was about sixteen or so. When I moved to the Lower East Side, it was the late '40s…1948. Where I lived is now a low-income project. It's a street called Willett Street. It's between Delancey and Rivington—67 Willett Street.

It was all walk-ups. We were on the top floor. There was four of us… four kids. It's not like I had to, but I was in the street all the time. Actually, the school was a block away, around the corner. After school we went to the community center, did arts and crafts, and then we'd come home and try to go out and play some more ball.

We'd come home for lunch; most of the mothers were home. Very few mothers worked. On the weekends, we'd play and hang out. We'd play in the park, mostly in the streets.

We had chores…take out the garbage, go to the store for my mother. But my sister did a lot of that stuff. My mother did the laundry. And since we were on the top floor, she'd string up a clothesline on the roof.

A recent photograph of George Boyd. *Courtesy of his son, Ernest Leif.*

My neighbors...at this time the Lower East Side was mostly Jewish and a few people of Catholic religion. Polish, Irish, Italian. Very few blacks in the area, very few. People were...hostile. But among the kids—at least in my vicinity—some of them were, but most of them weren't. As long as you know your own, they don't bother you. But then again, there's racism.

The kids on my block...it depends on what age it is...ten, eleven, twelve...we weren't involved in gangs. We're still too young for that. There were gangs there, but I wasn't involved in them, and there were some that were rougher than others. But I knew some people who were in gangs, and they kept an eye out for me.

I did go to church, but we went to a church in Harlem. We took the subway—the F train to the A. Those trains were underground. The Third Avenue El came down later, but we never took that one.

Dreams? It's hard because when you're young, you're changing all the time. You might want to be a baseball player, but by the time you get to high school you realize you don't have the ability to do this. Only thing you think about is going to school and maybe going to college and get a good job. By the time you're fifteen or sixteen years old, you're thinking, "When I finish high school, what am I going to do?" I don't know if anyone I knew at that time had any other dreams...like being a doctor. Maybe they did.

If you got sick, you went to the city hospitals, like Bellevue, Gouverneur. They took people in. My father didn't make a lot of money, so we went to a city hospital. The community center had a dental clinic; they didn't charge that much.

We had a fire escape—slept out there when it's hot. And you could see the other fire escapes, and people would be out there sleeping. That was in the summertime. Back then, it was fairly safe. You could just walk through the building and go out to the backyard. Some of them had fences, but most of them didn't. Between this building and that, you could just walk. If there was a fence, you'd just climb over it. Once we were hanging out in a place where we shouldn't have been, and the super came out and yelled, "Hey! Get out of here!" And the fences were small. We just jumped over them and scattered.

I finished high school and then I went to college. We moved from the Lower East Side at the time I graduated high school. I was basically on the Lower East Side for about seven years—from ten to seventeen. And then I came back again when I was about twenty-seven.

I wanted to live in Manhattan. The influence it had? At an early age, I became exposed to other cultures, all different kinds of people. The Lower

East Side was a mixed bag at that time. It gave me a perspective about this world, this society. In America, most of us grow up thinking we're all the same. I'm not saying it's bad or good. I'm just saying that's the way it is. Whether you read about things in life, it doesn't matter. I saw things firsthand. It gave me a perspective on how to view things.

In memoriam of Mr. George Boyd, who passed away in July 2010.

JACK DOWLING

Interviewed in January 2003 at Mr. Dowling's
apartment in Greenwich Village

M y mother was born in New York City, in Harlem on East 126th Street. Her father was an Austrian Jew; her mother was a Finn. It was a Finnish neighborhood at that time. They later moved to New Jersey, where my mother grew up, got married and where I was born. But the beat of New York harkened to me. I got a scholarship to Cooper Union when I was in high school, so I came to New York when I was about eighteen.

I didn't want to start going to Cooper Union right away, so I found a way to get out so I didn't lose my scholarship, and I went back two years later. In the meanwhile, I learned more about New York. More about art. More about the language of art...and was able to go back to class and have some understanding of what was going on around me.

I had an apartment at 64 St. Marks Place. It was five rooms on the top floor. The rent was nineteen dollars a month. The john was down the hall, of course. Had no heat. The kitchen stove was a regular gas stove, and the tub was in the kitchen—the standard Lower East Side railroad flat. I had five rooms, and the very back room had a door to the hall, so people could rent out a room if they wanted. Because the building was one story higher than my neighbors, I had windows on the side, which was very rare. And I could see out over rooftops from the apartment.

The superintendent of my building lived in the basement. He was Hungarian, and his wife was quite old at the time. He had...and I don't remember what the musical instrument is...but it filled his whole living room. It was something they'd brought with them from Hungary. It was

A view of Cooper Union from Astor Place in the late 1960s. *Courtesy of the Library of Congress.*

played like a piano, and he offered this to me because he didn't know what he was going to do with it and he was very old. But there was no way I could take it.

The neighborhood was filled with Polish, Hungarian, some Czech people. There were a few Puerto Rican families in some of the buildings. Not many, a few. In my building, the people who lived in the back on the other side of the hall were Spanish. But most everyone was Hungarian. The Polish were mostly on Seventh Street and Sixth Street, which meant that the neighborhood was scrubbed clean and the stoops were washed.

None of the students at Cooper Union lived in that area. Some lived in lofts on Bond Street or on Rivington and Allen Street. I had one friend who lived on East Sixth Street—a black woman. That was it. It was very quiet after ten thirty at night. There were no clubs. The restaurants all closed early. There were no shops selling tourist trinkets. There was no reason for anybody to stay open late.

Around the corner, there was a small Hungarian store, and they sold fresh black bread and tubs of cream cheese. And you would just buy it—ladle

During the 1930s, this Bowery restaurant offered five-cent meals. *Courtesy of the Library of Congress.*

it out as much as you wanted. So my Sunday mornings were always black bread and cream cheese and coffee and the newspaper. I have missed that the rest of my life.

There were a lot of small shops around. No supermarket that I can recall. There was one or two small restaurants tucked under stairways that were very cheap. You could have dinner for a dollar. I would eat out in these local restaurants...Hungarian...Polish.

There was a movie house around the corner on Second Avenue and Sixth Street. That became a big disco place years later—the Fillmore East. Across the street, on Second Avenue and Seventh Street, there was one movie theater that's been a legitimate off-Broadway theater for years. Down the street there was the Hebrew Loan Society. I know because I went there many times trying to get a loan when I was broke, which was often. I never had any luck. The Polish National Hall had a restaurant in there that later became the Electric Circus.

I went to school at night because I couldn't afford to go during the day. The jobs I had usually were pretty inconsequential. I did switchboard operator plug board—PBX boards, they were called. I could pick up a job in a few days as a PBX operator. And that was good. I worked everywhere from printing houses on Wall Street to the Copacabana to the docks of New York.

On my days off, I went over to the West Village. There wasn't much happening near me. It wasn't called the East Village then. That was a real estate invention. I liked my apartment; it was very simple. I had no furniture. I wasn't into decorating or fixing up. I really had nothing. I could move out with a suitcase and a couple of cartons of books. But I didn't really know anyone over there. I didn't meet Auden—W.H. Auden—until a number of years later. In 1958, in the spring, I met him through a friend. I graduated from school, and I was going to Europe. An old friend of Auden's insisted I should meet him before I went because he would tell me what to do in London. So we had a meeting at Auden's place on St. Mark's.

I used to go to Henry Street Settlement because at that time that was the only place—that and the Needle Trades High School—to see modern dance. Aside from Martha Graham, all the younger dance companies were there. You later saw these kind of companies at Judson Church.

Tompkins Square just seemed to be filled with a lot of old people sitting around in the sun. There were very few young people. But when that older generation died off, all those apartments became available. At the same time, the hippie movement began. Suddenly there was a lot of vacant space at a very cheap rent.

The Henry Street Settlement House today. *Courtesy of Eric Ferrara.*

The El was up...the Third Avenue El. That came down when I was in Europe...around '58 to '60. The Wanamaker Department Store—the great big building that runs between Eighth and Ninth Street and Broadway back to Astor Place—was as big as any of the big uptown department stores. It was out of Philadelphia, and it was handy for shopping for stuff you needed for the house. But it was a respected store—not cheap. It had good quality.

Where the parking lot is on Astor Place, where they're supposed to build some building now, there was a whole row of what they call taxpayers... one-story buildings. They were just small shops like cigar stores. They were torn down for that parking lot. [The parking lot was transformed into the high-rise "Sculpture for Living" in 2004.]

There were artists living along the Bowery in some of the lofts. I had a friend who had a loft on Bond Street. He paid the grand sum of $100 for rent. And I thought if I have to pay $100 I would have to go to work. And that was out of the question. The Bowery was the Bowery of Joseph Mitchell. It was exactly as he described—one cheap rooming house after another. And a lot of men who had nothing else in their lives. Many of them were born before the turn of the century, and they'd probably been drinking a good part of their lives.

It was quiet over there and incredibly safe. You had no concern about being on the street at any hour at any time. The front doors were always unlocked. The only thing that really startled me was that one night about one o'clock in the morning there was a knock on my door. And I opened the door to find a young lady standing there in her slip. I didn't invite her in, and I never discovered who she was or where she came from. But that was the highlight of 64 St. Marks Place.

I moved from there about 1954. A friend on Hudson and Horatio Street said the apartment next to him had become vacant. They had refurbished—put a toilet *in* the apartment. It was going to be a big leap from nineteen dollars to thirty-three dollars a month. But I figured I could do it.

On St. Marks Place, I heated with the kitchen stove, but it only heated the kitchen and the living room. Because the windows were in such bad shape, the place was always cold. Wait a minute. When I moved to Horatio Street, they didn't have heat. I heated that apartment with a coal stove. And the following year, the city made a law requiring these buildings to have steam heat. But at that time, none of the buildings had heat, only hot water. It was tough. There were a lot of fires. Coal stoves or kerosene. A lot of people would lose their electricity because they didn't pay the bill, and there'd be fires from candles.

Living on the Lower East Side…it was my first exposure to people who hadn't been born in this country, except for my grandparents. But my grandparents had become so Americanized that I forgot they hadn't been born in this country, even though they both spoke with slight accents. They very quickly got themselves away from their immigrant circles and moved to New Jersey. I found myself living in a neighborhood where people hadn't done that. They'd moved into neighborhoods where it was familiar, where they knew people from the "Homeland."

Many people didn't learn English…speak English. I hadn't had that kind of experience before. I was fascinated by other cultures. And when I went to Europe in the spring of 1958, I felt completely comfortable going into the unknown, meeting people who spoke different languages.

I could add…I met a young woman at a party uptown, and I took her on the Third Avenue El, which she'd never been on. And took her back to her Park Avenue apartment. And then one day, this young woman got away from her family. Wanted to see where I lived and came down in a car with a chauffeur and her fur coat. She came up the stairs and up the stairs and up the stairs 'cause I was six flights up. And she came to the apartment. And she was shocked. She couldn't believe that anybody could live this way. It was perfectly nice to go riding on the El but to come and see how a Bohemian actually lived was something else. And I never saw her again. So the Lower East Side made an impact on her, too.

Gladys Choma

Interviewed in August 2003 at the Sirovitch Senior Center, Twelfth Street and First Avenue

I was born in 1919 on Tenth Street, between Avenue C and D. My mother was born on Fourth Street between Avenue C and D, and my father, he was born in Brooklyn. His mother came from Germany. We spoke English. We never knew we were poor. We thought everybody was like us. We lived in the old tenements. On the first floor, there would be Italian families, then a Polish family. The bathroom was in the yard. In the hall, we had a commode. We had no heat. We had coal stoves, and we'd go in the street and find wood and bring it home; then we'd sit by the coal stove.

We shared everything. On Sunday, Mrs. Caboni would make meatballs, and to this day I can't find spaghetti that tastes like hers. She had eleven children. But she'd always give us a couple of macaronis. And my mother—if somebody came and needed biscuits, she'd give them. Biscuits were five cents a box then.

We did our shopping on the pushcarts, out in the streets. They started on Tenth Street and went to about Fifth Street. And they were downtown on Houston Street, but we never went there. To tell you the truth, I never went farther than Avenue B. There was no reason. And these peddlers, they would go to the market at four o'clock in the morning and then come back. And we had fresh vegetables just like we lived in the country. We never had bags; they'd wrap the vegetables in newspaper.

All the people that came from the different countries had bakeries. They used to have the fires in the basement; that's where they baked the bread and the cakes. We'd buy a roll for two cents. And we had a pickle stand right

A pushcart on Hester Street, circa 1896. *Courtesy of the Library of Congress.*

on the corner, and we'd get a pickle for a penny. That's one thing with poor people. Not that we had enough, but there was always food around.

My mom worked. Her first job was charwoman; she'd take care of the building and clean. In the summertime, we slept on the roof, and when it was real hot we sat in the street, downstairs on the stoop. And we slept on the fire escape. And when it would rain and we were sleeping on the roof, we'd all run. And we thought everyone lived like that.

Our church, Emmanuel Presbyterian Church, was on Sixth Street between Avenue C and D. They were very good to us. We'd have basketball games, and they had a sewing club. It was always open; we went every Sunday. I was baptized there. During the Depression...in '29...they'd give us a box of food once a week with potatoes, onions, whatever they had. And in the summer, we'd go to camp in Connecticut. Five dollars. Who could pay it? Most people couldn't.

I went to school right down on Ninth Street between Avenue B and C. And my school is still here between Avenue A and First Avenue...the junior high...on Twelfth Street. Tenth Street to Fifth Street was mostly Jewish. Then there'd be Polish and Eastern Europe. From Eleventh Street starting on Avenue B to First Avenue, it was Italian—that was their territory. From Fourteenth Street and Avenue C—now there's Stuyvesant Town there—to Eighteenth Street was Irish and German. And when we were children, if we went out of our territory, we'd say we were going uptown. I had relatives that lived on Sixteenth Street, so we're going to my cousin "uptown." We had relatives on Ludlow Street, so when we'd go to them, we were going downtown. Back then there were trolley cars. We never had five cents to go on a trolley car.

My father died when I was twelve years old. Before that, he used to work on the boats and the Lackawanna Railroad. At night, the tugboats would come in, and they'd dock on Tenth Street. We didn't have the East River Drive, we had docks. I used to swim here in the East River. My father was a watchman. Some of the boats that docked there, they'd have coal.

And the little boys…when my father wasn't looking, they'd go and steal some coal. We never had to lock our doors. We had one policeman; he used to watch us. He was on the beat. Not like now…in the cars. We weren't afraid of him. He watched us. He watched us good, too.

The iceman used to come around. We had an icebox, and we'd buy twenty-five cents of ice, and then we had to carry it up. We had a pan under there to catch the water, and how many times we forgot to empty the pan and we had a flood in the kitchen.

All our activities were at the church. Once or twice a year, we'd go to Central Park. They'd make us sandwiches with mayonnaise. Just plain mayonnaise. We had no peanut butter, nothing like that. And it was so good. After school, we came home. I was always with the children. I would babysit for no money. No one gave us anything. The mothers and the fathers, they were young; everybody around here got married fifteen, sixteen years old. So I'd tell 'em to go to the movies so I could watch their baby. I was so young my mother used to say, "Don't give her the baby carriage. She can't reach the handle." My father…my whole family…we all loved children.

My father loved to dance. He taught us all how to dance. And we were the first ones to get a radio, so my friends used to come, and my father would put it on. We were the first ones to have a Victrola. Records were three for five dollars. You'd wind it up. We danced at home.

My mother lost two children…passed away. So I had a brother and a sister. My brother, he went to the Second World War and came back. When I got married, I got my own apartment on Tenth Street and Avenue C. It was on the fourth floor, and it was one room. There was a wall between the bedroom and the kitchen. We had no heat, no hot water. The toilet was in

Children playing on the street, circa 1910. *Courtesy of the Library of Congress.*

the hall. And I paid nine dollars a month in 1936. I had three children—two girls and a boy. They used to call me the "Gypsy." They'd say, "Where does she live now?" At that time, you could move; there was rooms…now they call them apartments.

Many landlords…if you rent a room they'd paint for you, and they'd put linoleum on the floor, and the rent was eighteen dollars. So I moved twenty-two times. It would be one building here, then around the corner. The farthest I went was to Eighth Street. One apartment I moved into, they painted it the wrong color, and I moved out. Did you ever hear of such a crazy thing?

My husband was a longshoreman, and when we first got married, he would go six o'clock in the morning; they used to call it "shape up" on the docks. They'd stand in a circle, and the boss would pick them out. Most of the time he'd get work. If they didn't pick him, he'd go back three o'clock for the night shift. They had it hard.

Then they hired him permanently, and he became a shop steward. He was for the union.

Thirty-eight years my husband worked for the company. And he passed away in 2000, and he was eighty-seven. I'm eighty-four. My children—the three of them went to college. I have one in Rhode Island…that's my son.

My girl is in Michigan. She married a minister. My other girl is in Florida. Now I'm on Twelfth Street and Avenue C in Haven Plaza. I would never go to Florida. I can't stand the heat. My girl in Florida calls me at least three times a day. At night she puts me to sleep.

When I was growing up, my dreams were to get married and have ten, twelve children.

I love children. I love to cook. My mother-in-law taught me a lot about foreign food. I learned to cook it. You'd think we were born in Europe. We had the best food. We were so poor, but you couldn't find finer food than we had on the East Side. We never knew how poor we were. But it was a good life…a very good life. And I hope the Lord will keep me. I don't want to go any place. I don't think I could live any place else.

SIDNEY FERMAGLICH

Interviewed in March 2005 at Mr. Fermaglich's
apartment on Grand Street

My name is Sidney Fermaglich. You know how to spell it? F-E-R…M-A-G…L-I-C-H. My family was from Austria…Croatia. Somewhere in Austria. I was born here; my oldest brother was born here. If he was alive, he'd be over a hundred. I'll be ninety in December. I got a baby brother who's going to be eighty. My mother had six children—all boys. First I lived at 51 Sheriff Street. Then we moved to 65 Sheriff Street. Then we moved to the fancy one on 67 Sheriff Street, where we had our own toilet and bath. And November 1930, we moved here, into the Amalgamated on Grand Street. My father took five rooms. The rent was $62.50 a month. This was during the Depression.

I went to school at P.S. 34. It was right here on Sheriff and Broome. And then I went to P.S. 22 on Sheriff and Stanton [and then] P.S. 97 for junior high school. From there I went to Seward Park, and then I got out of there and I went to work.

When I got home from school, I'd ask my mother to cut me a slice of bread with some *shmear* on it. It was a treat. Then I went downstairs and played ball or did crazy things that the kids would do. At times we broke into a peddler's stand and stole sweet potatoes. We'd put them on the fire. We made a fire out of what we called our "election fire." We saved up, and we got crates and boxes, and on election day we made a big bonfire. Then we went down to the Forward Building and watched the results come in. We made the fire, but I don't recall who was mayor.

The entrance to Seward Park High School in 2012. *Courtesy of Eric Ferrara.*

When I was little...the games. It was rough games. We were East Side kids, and we played whatever we got a hold of. It was a very interesting street. The hoodlums that hung around there...the boys. They were tough.

I had a great time as a kid. It was a different time. I used to run the whiskey for the bootlegger that lived downstairs. He gave me a half a dollar every time I made a trip. A half a dollar to me was like a million dollars. Whadda ya' think? You bought a piece of candy for a penny or two; you went to a movie for about ten cents. Especially with the Depression. I went to all the movie theaters. All of them. I went to Loew's on Delancey Street; I went to Loew's on Fifth Street and Avenue B; I went on Clinton Street to the Odeon; the Palace; the Apollo. On Rivington Street, they had the Waco. We used to call it the "Ranch House." You went in there for a nickel. I joined the "Edgies"...the Educational Alliance. I went to camp...I was a kid there.

We didn't have bathtubs where we lived. We had a sink in the kitchen, and you washed up in the kitchen. There was a bathhouse at 62 Sheriff Street called Gang's. It was owned by a man whose name was Gang. That was his name. He was my neighbor. You took a bath, and you slept over; they

Children playing leapfrog, circa 1915. *Courtesy of the Library of Congress.*

had cots. There was more than one bathhouse. At 65 Sheriff Street—in the basement—they put in some bathtubs, and we used to go in there to bathe. For a quarter, a half a dollar, you took a bath. On Rivington and Allen... they had showers and baths there. That was for free. Today, you turn the faucet on, you get all the water you want. Then it was different.

The people on my block were all Jews. A few Gentiles. The Jews were merchants...the butcher...the man that sold chickens...merchants. I didn't go to synagogue. My father wasn't religious. I came from a nonreligious family. My mother didn't work; she raised five, six sons. My father was what they call today a salvage man...a junk man. He made a good living. Very good man; the best man I ever saw in my life. Went around, and he'd buy junk...metal...rags. That's what he did, and he sorted it and sold it. He had a junk store at 109 East Second Street and a horse and wagon. The horse's name was Charlie. In those days, my father used to bring home the junk...the salvage. Certain pieces of wood—we put them in the stove, and we heated the apartment.

It was a very interesting street. Right opposite us, at 64 Sheriff Street, lived the Greenglasses. They lived on the first floor. Ethel...she married Rosenberg. And she'd be my age now if she were alive. She went to Seward Park High, but we never socialized. A girl who's fifteen is looking for older fellows. She didn't bother with us kids. She was a nice person...very nice.

They came from a large family, too. The oldest was Sammy. He was as old as my oldest brother. Then they had Bernie. I don't know if he's around or not. Then they had David, who turned her in, if you remember the case. He married a girl by the name of Price. They wanted to prosecute her, so he turned his sister in. It was a terrible time.

The father, Bernie, was a mechanic...a machinist. He had a little machine shop right at 64 Sheriff Street. And the mother was the custodian of the building. She was a tough, hardworking woman. That was the Greenglass family.

As far as I was concerned, they were all nice people. Whatever you want to think of them—may she rest in peace—she was a fine girl. It was unfortunate.

The last time I was on Sheriff Street was when they electrocuted Ethel. I went to give her mother what they call a *Kugel*. Everybody deserted her. They were called rats, spies, whatever. And I loved these people. I thought a hell of a lot differently. Maybe I'm a leftist, I don't know. I'm telling you the truth. The night that they electrocuted her, I went down there. It was a rough time. I know most of the people on the block condemned them. I don't know why. The other children in the family were hardworking, good mechanics.

I grew up in a very privileged home. My brothers went to college. The oldest one graduated from Columbia. My late brother graduated from NYU. In those days, a lot of kids didn't even finish high school. I finished high school; went into the army. After the war, I came back here. That was in 1945, the end of World War II.

I went into business, my father's business. I went bankrupt in the business. Not all success stories, believe me. I got married. I got the apartment. It was very comfortable. It still is comfortable here.

I got lovely neighbors. I got one, she gave me the *Purim*. I think I left it on the table in there. They're religious people. I don't bring pork in the house or any non-kosher food, but I'm not religious. And my daughter comes up every Thursday to take care of me. She lives across the street. My granddaughter comes up once in a while.

The people I grew up with…I don't think they're around. All my friends—my contemporaries—they're all gone. They lived to eighty…seventy-eight. I'm still around. How long, I don't know. And I don't care. I've lived my life. I've got no regrets. My childhood was terrific. I did all the things kids did. I was a bully. There were people that didn't like me. I wasn't a nice kid. I look back, and I did a lot of bad things. But most of us kids were like that.

My name…Fermaglich. It means wealth. You understand Yiddish? Pronounce it the way I do…FER…MA…GLICH…That means "wealth."

ANITRA FRAZIER

*Interviewed in September 2001 at a coffee shop on
Twenty-fifth Street and Sixth Avenue*

I'm speaking about the Lower East Side, where I lived beginning in 1958. I was twenty-two years old, and I had just graduated from college.

But that summer, I got a job in summer stock at North Shore Music Theatre in Beverly, Massachusetts, singing, dancing and acting. And halfway through that summer, I knew it. I wanted to be in show business. And I was determined...I'm going to New York. And I saved my pennies like crazy.

When I came to New York, I was very concerned about money because my family was horrified that I was going into show business. So I couldn't ask them for help, and I had about $300. So my friends said the Lower East Side is where the apartments are the cheapest...but you can't live there. "Oh yes I can," said I.

And down I went to the Lower East Side. I found an apartment on the first floor on East Fourth Street between First Avenue and Avenue A. It was one room. There was one of these really old gas stoves; there was no heat and no hot water. I had this kind of closet area where there was a sink and a toilet. And this was wonderful that I had my own toilet in my own apartment. Not one in the hallway. But the tub was in the kitchen; it was up on legs. And there was this big metal cover on it that you used for counter space.

I didn't want to use the gas stove too much because you'd have to pay the gas bill, and I had to pay a telephone bill because I had to have a telephone to get work as an actress. So I'd go out at night

Anitra Frazier on East Fourth Street in 2012. *Courtesy of Eric Ferrara.*

into the alleys and look for firewood to put in the fireplace. And I ate lamb's liver. At that time, it was twenty-nine cents a pound. I knew enough about nutrition to know it was very rich in protein and minerals and vitamins.

My fiancé, Joe, followed me to New York, and we'd sleep together in my apartment. Joe said it was better to put the mattress up off the floor. The way to do this was you put your mattress on a door propped up on bricks at each corner. So I'd gone out to the alley and had found discarded bricks. And he knew where there were doors. Well, these doors were solid oak; they were heavy. And so the two of us carried one of these doors all the way across town.

And just as we got to Second Avenue, there was the green grocer on the corner. And he was selling beets. And he wrung the neck off the beets and took the greens and threw them in the trash. And without thinking, I said, "What are you doing with your greens?"

He looked down at these two young kids carrying this door, looking like *La Boheme,* and he said, "I'm not doing anything with them, honey." And he put them in a bag, and he gave me extra greens, and he said, "Listen, I'll give you greens any time you want." So I had lamb's liver and beet greens, which we cooked on the open fireplace so we didn't have to use the gas. We did have electricity. We had electric lights.

The night Joe proposed, we were on the mattress, on the door, on the bricks, with the fireplace burning low. The air very cold. Us huddled under the blankets. I used my coat as a blanket. And I swear, he proposed to me. And he was very persuasive. He had a job. He was a baritone soloist at Riverside Church, for which he got, I believe, $125 a week, which was a huge sum. I was working at Papermill Playhouse and was getting $135 a week.

We went to St. Luke's Church on Hudson Street, and on the wedding day the priest was there…but no Joe! Then Joe came running in all out of breath, saying, "I got us another apartment! We have heat and hot water."

What he didn't say was it was five flights up. And instead of being $27 a month, it was $35 a month. I said, "My God. What's going to happen if we're both out of work?"

We were both in show business. And every time we had an audition, we had to leave a picture, our name and telephone number. And every time I left my number, I was embarrassed because my exchange…down there on the Lower East Side, which was supposed to be very disreputable. It was "CANAL."

So when Joe came and said, "I've got this wonderful apartment, it's three rooms, it's heated, it's got hot water." I said, "Wait. What's the telephone exchange?" And he said, "Let me see...SWAMP 7." And for a minute, I believed him.

On Fourth Street, the garbage cans were outside the window, and the bums from the Bowery would rummage through the cans at night. I found the bums to be nice, quiet people. At night, I'd get off the train on Second Avenue and then walk uptown, and they'd be standing around. And back in those days, if a man slept on the street, someone would call the police. The cops had an arrest quota. And if they had to fill their quota, they'd just run in a bum. One of the charges was "accosting" a lady...accosting means "speaking to." Of course, in those days a lot of people smoked, including me. The bums all smoked. And I'd look around to make sure there were no cops watching, and I'd give them a pack of matches and a couple of cigarettes. And they were kind of protective. If a new bum was there and didn't know—or he was drunk—an older guy would say, "Hey, that's a lady. Leave her alone."

My neighbors on Fourth Street...I didn't see them much except for the green grocer. He was a Jewish man in his thirties, and he was on the corner of Second Avenue and Fourth Street with a pushcart with all these vegetables. The man probably pushed it all the way from Delancey to uptown...We were considered uptown at Fourth Street.

When I came home, I was dead tired. In the morning, I'd dress, put on my makeup, pick up my music and off I'd go. I had dance class, voice lessons, auditions. Sometimes I'd stop at Klein's to pick up a bargain. And when I came home, I had to quickly change into blue jeans and go out and look for firewood.

We were big on folk singing and guitars at that time. They were playing guitars in Washington Square. There was the Bitter End and the Village Gate, and we'd go there. This was in the early '60s. And Joe ended up in the Chad Mitchell Trio, which was a folk singing group traveling all over the place. I had a Broadway show. We'd go down to the Village Gate and watch the improvisations—Allen Arkin, Barbara Harris...marvelous improvs they would do. Also the Bitter End...the folk singers. I remember meeting John Denver before John Denver was ever known.

The Lower East Side...it was a jumping-off place to get my career started. It allowed me to say this is what I want to do, and it allowed me to succeed. I was able to eat. I had a roof over my head. It was cheap. It was marvelous. And all these dairy restaurants. Who had ever heard of a dairy restaurant? Borscht...I never heard the word "borscht" in my life. I had never had sour cream. If the cream was sour, you threw it out. It broadened me.

James Galuppo

Interviewed in December 2004 at Mr. Galuppo's factory, Etna Tool and Die Corporation, on Bond Street near the Bowery

I grew up on the Lower East Side. I was born on Madison Street in 1918. It's still there—33...33 Madison Street. I don't know what it was like 'cause I was born there. I didn't stay there long because we moved to Oliver Street—54 Oliver Street. The only reason that street was famous is because we had a senator there. He was born on Oliver Street too.

My family—my mother and father were born here, but my grandmother and grandfather were born in Italy. One set was born in Potenza—Potenza is the ankle—that's my mother's side. My father's side, I think it was Sala Consalina. They came here because coming from an agricultural background, they worked for peanuts. They worked hard; they didn't make anything. And here the streets are made of gold, right?

So they came here. And my mother and father were born here. And I was born here, too. My father was a bricklayer. He was in that field...construction. My mother was a housewife. I got two brothers and one sister. The first school I went to was P.S. 1, and from there I went to Harran High School on Tenth Avenue and Fifty-something Street. And that's as far as my schooling went. I didn't go to college. I thought I was too smart for college. The teachers said there wasn't much they could put in my head, so I assumed that I was too smart.

From Oliver Street, I went to Oak Street. And Oak Street was a very nice street. It was communal. A lot of boys there, young boys. And it was fun, you know; we had baseball teams. There weren't that many girls for some reason...only a handful of girls. We played ball all the time. After

James Galuppo outside his shop on Bond Street. *Courtesy of Eric Ferrara.*

school…we had teams. We played against each other because every block had a team.

There weren't any parks nearby. When we played ball for money we'd go down to Peck's Slip. Down by Water Street, near the fish market. Beautiful streets there…wide and all. And we'd make the bases and all that stuff there. We didn't play stick; we played punch ball. You had to punch the ball by hand. And we'd play for money. We could win twelve, fourteen dollars. And we'd go around and take bets…get a nickel…a dime. And if we won, we'd double the money. See what I mean? So everybody was praying that we win.

I lived on 34 Oak Street. It was six stories. I lived on the fifth floor. It was like railroad rooms. No heat. We had to make our own. I had to go looking for wood. We had a coal fire. And when we had enough money to buy coal, we used coal. If we didn't have enough money, we used wood. So we froze to death. We had three or four of us in one bed hanging on to each other. It was fun.

The bathroom was in the hall. In some of the buildings the bathroom wasn't even in the hall; it was in the yard. So you had to go to the yard. The water, in those days. They did have plumbing, but there were no tubs. No showers. Nothing like that. We had the Cherry Street Baths. We used to go to wash up…clean up. It was nice, but it was public.

We'd go once or twice a week. Today, you take a shower every day, you know what I mean. I don't know why. In those days, you took a shower about twice a week. And depending on what kind of work you had…if you had dirty work, then it was different. But for young children, they had big tubs where they watched us.

My grandmother had sixteen children. But out of sixteen children, only twelve survived. Why? If you got the whooping cough or the measles—that was it. You could die from small things. It was painful to go through. There were doctors. Our doctor was Dr. Manny. Fortunately, he took most of the people that could pay him. The doctor's fees were two dollars. We went there to get medicines. He had an office on Oliver Street. He was very nice to us.

Shopping? We didn't have shopping malls. We just had plain stores here and there. The Greeks had their stores. The Spanish had their stores. Italians had their stores. It depends on what you wanted to get. You'd go to a Greek place; you'd get plenty of olives, cheese, stuff like that. And the Italians had bakeries. Bakeries were a separate enterprise. You always went to a bakery for bread. That's what it was. It was not…like today…shopping centers. Meat? You had to go to a butcher shop. Today, everything is in one place.

James with his parents, Anna and John Galuppo, and his baby brother, Michael, on Madison Street in the 1920s. *Courtesy of James Galuppo.*

Portrait of James Galuppo's family, circa 1920. *Courtesy of James Galuppo.*

Neighbors? Right across the way my aunt lived up there with her twelve children. They didn't fool around. And then the neighbors on the side…number 36 Oak Street…that was another six-story building, and we knew everybody in there. It was a community because people knew everybody. You looked out the window, and you said hello.

The street was mostly Italian. If you went to the next block, it was mostly Spanish. If you went to another block, there were Greeks. If you went to Oliver Street, then you had a lot of Irish. This was in the '20s.

Church? Everybody went to church. The guys would get together, "OK, who's going to church?" And a whole bunch of boys would go to church. We went to a church on Catherine Street, which is still there. I went every Sunday. My mother would kill me if I didn't.

The movies were my second home because on a Saturday or Sunday we'd stay there. You went to the movies about ten o'clock, and you wouldn't get out until about three. The kids just sat there 'cause in those days you had double features—comedy, news and comics. So it was at least three or four hours. And all this for ten cents.

We went to the Chatham Square Theatre. The one who owned it was a Jewish woman; her name was Mazie. She was a character. And we'd go there, and it was ten cents to get in. But if we had two people, we'd go like this, "Mazie…can we get two for fifteen?"

And she'd say, "Get out of here! Leave me alone!" and all that stuff. And then she'd go, "Ah, come on in." And then they'd come around. They sold pretzels…two pretzels for five cents. And we were munching on them. We enjoyed ourselves. Because we knew everybody. Theater was fun. Because we'd sit there for hours. Fifteen cents for the two of us. It was a past time…a very nice past time.

In those days, there was welfare, but not like today. Welfare was if you could prove that the head of the family was earning less than fifteen dollars a week. When you got that little, they would help you out with a bag of coal. They'd give you a couple of boxes of prunes, I don't know why. A couple of cans of meat, which was probably buffalo…that they shot out West. Very stringy, poor-quality meat. And my mother made meatballs because that's the only way you could eat it…grind it up. And then they'd give you butter. They didn't overdo it. If that's what they had, that's what they gave you.

Nothing like today; you go to the supermarket, and you take out what you want. You know? But that's what it was. We did the best we could. And things were cheaper in those days.

James on the Coney Island boardwalk in the 1920s. *Courtesy of James Galuppo.*

Basically, it was a communal thing. You'd look out the window and see your neighbor across the way and say, "Hey. How are ya?" Everybody knew each other. You live in a high-rise today, you don't know anybody. And getting together with people in a high-rise is a big deal. Years ago it wasn't. People knew each other. We had block parties…dancing and a stand where you could buy corn or soda. They had a little music, and you could dance with the girls there. It was very nice.

In 1942, I was a big boy. They grabbed a hold of me and sent me to Panama. I had a job in a machine factory. And when I got back, I pursued my same trade…I went into business and manufactured tools and dyes for artificial flowers. I found the tool and dye business had an ethic. It was hard work. You had to know what you were doing.

Growing up on the Lower East Side—first of all—it was fun. Of course, in those days the only thing you thought about was to make money—to live, to survive, a job. That was it. If you had a good job, it was a big deal. Of course, there was a lot of unemployment.

Nobody owned property; nobody owned a house. But today, people have more and more than they had in those days. My grandmother and grandfather worked hard, and they had nothing. At least we worked hard and we have a little bit. We didn't get to be multi-multimillionaires, but we did a lot better than they did. They had nothing, but they were happy.

I'm still working because I like to work. And may God give me health. What do you do in twenty-four hours? Eight hours you sleep; you got sixteen hours to go. So what do you do in sixteen hours? You got to do something.

Joyce Kanowitz

Interviewed in January 2001 at a coffee shop on
Fourteenth Street and Sixth Avenue

I came to the Lower East Side in 1955 from London, England. What happened was, I'd always wanted to visit America. I also wanted to visit other places in the world, but my father said, "Why don't you go to New York; the whole world is in New York." And that year my father died. I took a leave of absence from work, got a ticket on a charter plane to New York. When I got here, I stayed with my aunt until she threw me out.

I finally got an apartment of my own, which was really two old rooms over a synagogue on Henry Street and Montgomery. I loved to lay in bed on Saturday morning and hear the singing from the synagogue.

I found the Lower East Side a very warm place to live in. I think what it was, I was born in the Jewish ghetto in London, and I remember the warmth and the closeness. Everybody knew everybody.

It was around 1955. The area was mostly Jewish, but there were a lot of Chinese down the street. There were old garages that the rag people used. This old man had a rag place there, and he called it his "CCC"—"Cold and Cruel Cellar." He was very nice, and he gave me furniture. He had professional children living on Long Island. But he didn't want to go to them. This was his life, and this is where he stayed .

He sold the rags to a commercial place. They were converted to material or paper. And Joseph Papp. He had a cellar filled with rags. His father had been a rag merchant, and he inherited his father's rag business. When I met him, he said, "I have this great dream. I want to bring Shakespeare to the people." And I said, "Go ahead. Why not?" And he said, "I have to persuade

Joyce Kanowitz on Henry Street in 2012. *Courtesy of Nina Howes.*

the city to let me use a park." And I said, "How about the park down the road? This is where the people are." And he did. His very first performance was that park off Grand Street, by the river. It's like an amphitheatre.

My flat...I loved it. I could look out my back window and see a greenhouse; it used to be an old mansion. Originally, merchants had built houses there, all along East Broadway. When you came in the flat, the fireplace was facing you—that was the means of heat. But it was illegal. I remember once the landlord came to see the apartment. I knew that I wasn't supposed to have a fire in the apartment, so I had had a fire all night—this was wintertime—and I put it out. Swept up the fireplace. Hid everything. He came in, and he looked around. His assistant touched the fireplace, and he knew, but he didn't say anything.

Everything I needed for the house I found in the street. I found an old zinc tub, scrubbed it up. And that's how I bathed—in front of the fireplace. It was lovely, and it was really sexy when you had friends in. "Just a minute dear, I have to take a bath." There was a water heater there. I remember the pipes were rusty, so you had to run the water for a long time; otherwise, the water was rusty. Somebody who lived there before had put this in.

The landlord didn't do anything. Nothing. Just collect the rent. I think mine was twenty-one dollars a month. However, I was only able to earn about ten dollars a day at that time. And then they deducted money for food, so you came home with eight dollars a day.

I worked in the day care center on Second Avenue and Houston. And the big one on East Broadway, a big settlement house. It was interesting 'cause there were Jewish children who spoke Yiddish, Chinese children who spoke Chinese. I worked with three-year-olds, and there were Latino children who spoke Spanish. So these little Chinese kids, I remember they'd sit at the table and they say, "Carne, carne, carne."

On Henry Street...I went to the community center around the corner—the Henry Street Settlement. I'd go almost every night and make pottery. They let me do it for nothing. I just walked in one day and said, "Gee, I'd love to be able to work on this." People were so nice.

On the weekends, I hung out in the Village, off Sixth Avenue around McDougal. McDougal in those days was the heart of the Village; it was small. It wasn't honky-tonk. It wasn't like it is today. It was beats; it was poets. In the cafés, there were poetry readings and art exhibits.

I went to jazz clubs. I remember going to one place. I was sitting at a table, drinking wine, and after the show the band invited me up to Harlem, where they really played. I had no idea where I went, but it was okay.

No, that was the strange thing…being out late at night. It was OK. The streets were alive. I used to walk down Broadway and along Canal Street, and then I'd always stop at this luncheonette on the corner. I think it was called Joe's. I always stopped there, had something—a coffee, whatever. And then walked on. I never thought to take transport. Being European, there were certain things you didn't spend money on. If you had legs, you walked. I felt safe. The only thing I knew about, there was pot around. You could smell it, but I was never part of that scene.

I'm no great beauty, but I got so many marriage proposals because there were a lot of guys who liked women who were up front. I ended up with the best one…Rubin. We moved in to an apartment which had a bathroom and had heat. Had radiators that came on for two hours in the morning and two hours in the evening.

That was on Madison Street. We lived there until we decided to get married, and we moved to Brooklyn. But it was funny because Rubin had told the landlady that I was his sister. When we decided to move, he tells her, "My sister's getting married and moving to Canada." And she said, "I'm so

The sign for the Henry Street Settlement House in 2012. *Courtesy of Eric Ferrara.*

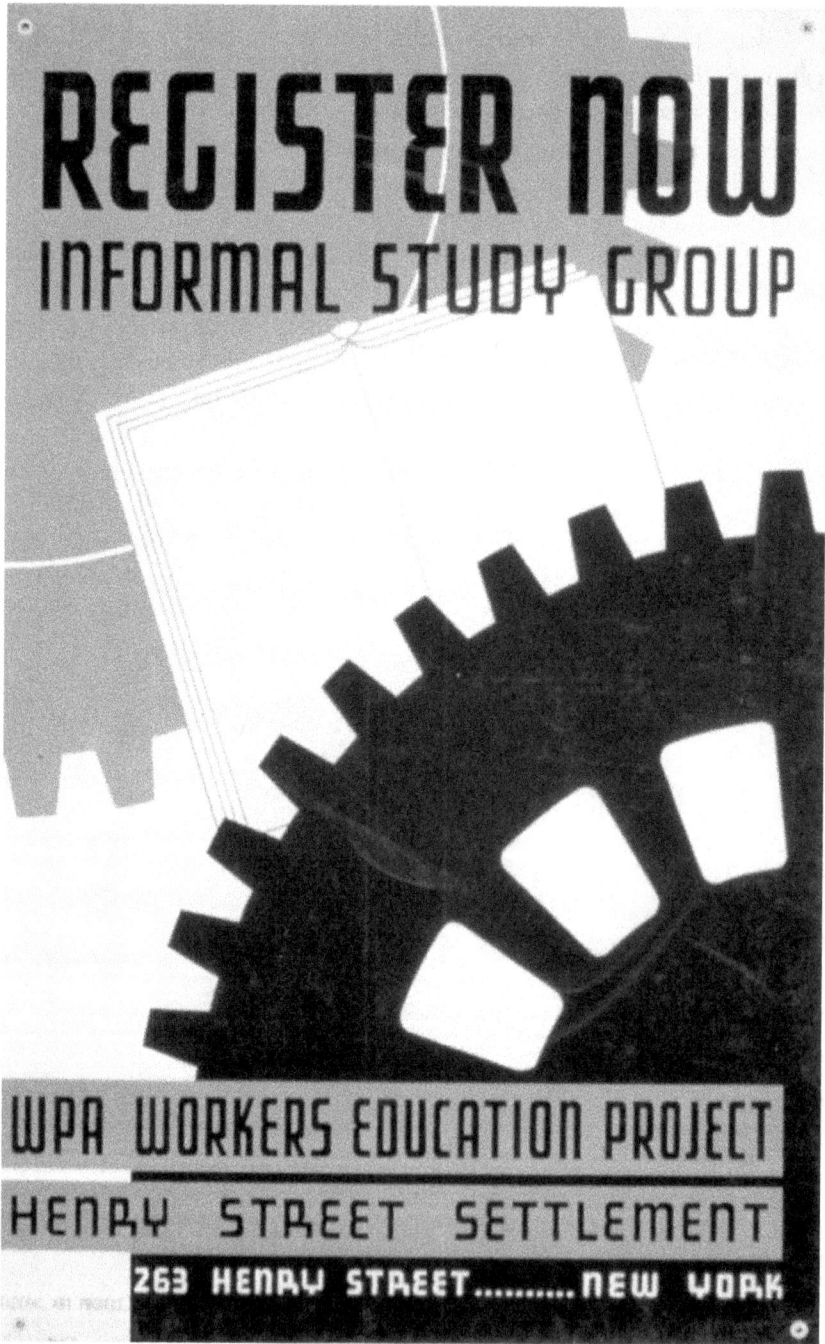

A 1940 poster for a WPA workshop at the Henry Street Settlement House. *Courtesy of the Library of Congress.*

glad you two decided to get married. You shouldn't be living like this. You should be married and have children." So she knew all along.

And she was so cute, the way she blushed.

I wasn't an immigrant in the sense of coming here to better my path. It was a personal thing. I was rather biased against Americans like a lot of young Europeans in those days. Americans would come to Europe. They had all the money, they had all the nice clothes. It wasn't that we were poor, but we were still suffering from the ravages of the war. We had rationing at least five years after the war ended. There wasn't a lot of food, and clothing was rationed. We signed up for a refrigerator, a tiny refrigerator. It took us five years to get to the top of the list. That's how things were postwar.

So I said I've got to get rid of this prejudice, this bias. I should go to America and see. When I came to New York City, I felt there was an outburst of creativity in experimental work. It was all here. My father was right. The other thing I felt was I didn't feel Jewish. Separated, apart, as we were in Europe, in London. There was always, "Oh, you're Jewish? You don't look Jewish. How interesting." It was like a curiosity, being Jewish. Everybody here appeared to be speaking Yiddish…I think what it was.

I was mixing in with the art and theatrical people who use a lot of Yiddish words. A *shtick* and a this. I didn't feel oppressed as a Jew here. It was OK to be Jewish. Whereas in England, I didn't deny I was Jewish, but I was guarded about it. I remember my father fighting with the Blackshirts, as they were called…the fascists. They would come into the Jewish ghetto and hold street meetings. This was prior to the war, and we used to have to pull him away. My father was a little guy, and these guys were big beefy guys, and the cops would just stand there. Wouldn't do anything.

Lydia Krushelnytsky

*Interviewed in March 2001 at the Ukrainian National Home
at 140 Second Avenue*

I am from the Ukraine. My family came here in '49, my whole family. That means we split; my father, my mother, my two brothers; they [came to America first], and they went to New Jersey, where there are friends to take care of them. They came about, I think, one half a year earlier.

First thing, I was crying all night, my first night here, because people talk. We can't have our luggage because we will pay duties, so put everything on…then you will pay nothing. If they find extra you will pay duties.

We didn't have money. We came by ship to Boston, so I put on everything what I had, not to pay duties. It was tenth August 1949; it was very, very hot. After trip from Europe, we are going by train to New York. In the train it was very hot, so I went to the ladies' room and to fresh myself a little bit with water; everything was wet, so I put everything from myself to the pocketbook and came out.

Then we came to New York, and a friend of my husband's—he was a lawyer—was waiting for us, from Catholic Action. We were helped to come here by Catholic Action. It was such a group that was bringing Catholics after the war. So we came here, and we went [by taxicab] to the Twenty-third Street MCA—you know YMCA, I call it "MCA"—so we went there, and the taxicab stopped. That lawyer came out. My son, who was about seven years old, fell asleep in the taxicab. So I took him, leaving my pocketbook. The lawyer closed the door; the taxicab with everything what I took from myself, all papers, everything, took off.

An early portrait of Lydia Krushelnytsky. *Courtesy of the Estate of Lydia Krushelnytsky.*

A more recent photograph of Lydia Krushelnytsky. *Courtesy of the Estate of Lydia Krushelnytsky.*

We were running after the cab. I didn't forget…just I wanted to take first my son and then pocketbook. So I lost everything. I was crying all night. Because not of material value, but they were all sentimental value…more value than material. Of course, it was everything gold and so on. But I was crying. I was so hurt. You know that feeling…I lost something what was tying me up to my life. My ring after graduating high school and so on and so on. My engagement bracelet from my husband—everything. So I lost everything. And you know we came, but finally we are all together.

So we find some apartment; it was some place near Delancey, over there. And we started to be there together and started to look for work. I found the fifth day…fifth day! After fifth day coming here, I found a job in the sewing factory. It was very, very good place because they were doing for Lord and Taylors, and there was another store on Fifth

Avenue, doesn't exist anymore, very famous. So we were sewing for that…suits…coats.

The factory was in Queens. I was near Delancey, but I would travel. I took the subway every day. So I was sewing there for ten years. I didn't know how to sew. One time I was sewing, they gave me this skirt and told me to sew. I was trying to ask somebody, back and forth, "How do you sew this?" "What do you mean?" "Isn't it all the same?"

"No my dear." He showed me how to sew…I didn't know even from what side to start. I think the hours were from eight to five or six. You know, he said, you do nice job. Sometime the cut on the suit is not even. I was fixing the corners. So I did that. I was sewing patterns; they teach me to do patterns. That was my job.

So it was very pleasant. The only thing, the table where we were sitting was next to the presses and the steam from pressing machine. You know I was sweating. I was wet from head to shoe. After work, I change, then run to do ballet classes and to do rehearsals. At St. George's School…they had gym with a stage…but at that time it was small school, not what it is now.

At first we were living off Delancey Street; it was across…I forgot the street…it doesn't exist anymore, that's why I forgot. They have new buildings there. Delancey when you go to the bridge, the Williamsburg Bridge—it's on the right side. It was maybe two years we lived over there downtown, and then in about '53 we moved to Tenth Street and corner Avenue B, where the park is. The corner building. And then we moved to First Avenue between Sixth and Seventh Street where we live till now.

We did our shopping on Avenue C…food shopping. They had, you know, carts, and were selling all that. I remember my mother; she didn't know English. I knew English a little bit when I came here. I studied in Europe a little bit. She didn't. And she came, and I was writing for her, translating her the words. And she said to this one Jewish man that was selling from this cart, "Why don't you talk in our language. Our language! What is it? Everybody from other country." And she was going back speaking Ukrainian to everybody. She never learned English…never learned English.

My parents were with us, and we never let them work. We decided. My brother was physician; after a year, he made his board. My husband was lawyer. But first my husband and him, they were cleaning in the hotels, cleaning the bathrooms—all jobs you could get.

Then we start to build everything here, including this building…Second Avenue and Ninth Street…on the corner…Veselka…this building if you go to Second Avenue, next one is Ukrainian National Home. My husband was running to get the shares to buy the building. We all did our best for this Ukrainian Youth Organization, Sport Club. Then between Seventh and Sixth Street is our credit union. That's all we did.

Everything is what's done with our money and our hard work. Not only this building was built, but we bought beautiful, in the mountains, beautiful summer camp. We bought another youth organization that is still on Second Avenue. We built everything. We built school, we built church. St. George is built with our money. Who would give it money? I worked all day at the sewing factory, went to rehearsals at night and then going to the Women's Association because we were in association. We had Ukrainian Museum on Second Avenue, between Twelfth and Thirteenth Street. Go and see. And we organized here the Shevchenko society on Fourth Avenue between Ninth and Tenth Street. It's for our great poet, Taras Shevchenko. [The Ukrainian Museum is now in a new facility at 222 East Sixth Street.]

A sense of community among the Ukrainians? Yes…I'll tell you what. It's easy to explain it. We came from the same country, and almost 60–70 percent of us knew each other. Like my husband, he came. "Look, my choir is here."

From the theater we knew [each other] from the old country; from the high schools, from the universities, people knew us. That's why we started to do something—to organize. So we organized a lot of societies; a society that was responsible for all our…how do you say…each one belongs to one.

We wanted to take part in normal life like we used to have in our country. That was our goal. And school for our children so they learn Ukrainian besides the English. Ukrainian courses Saturdays still we have. So I think we did everything what was possible…to higher our standards, to send children to the university.

We are proud that we had such a good opinion in community…not stealing…not killing…not using narcotics. You know what I think…and I think it's very big…how do you say…factor in it. It is family life.

And when I work…here, there, in factory, in theater…I always had time for my son.

On the night of classes for small children…always mother is bringing them, waiting for them, picking them up. It's feeling of belonging to the family. I think when you have feeling to belong to the family, you develop feeling to belong to society, to nation. I am not American by birth, but I think it's the wonderfulest country in the world.

JAN LEE

Interviewed in February 2012 at NomWah Tea Parlor on Doyers Street

My father was born here on Mott Street to a midwife. His father was born in Toishan, China, a city-state within Guangdong Province. The dialect is related to Cantonese, but many Cantonese speakers don't understand Toishanese. It's like someone from Louisiana speaking Creole. You can understand some English words, but it's hard. As far as we know, my grandfather came here in 1890.

He worked for an import/export company. He could read and write; this was unusual. Most of the men were illiterate. But he'd gone to school in the local village when he was back in China. And because his mother needed documents translated, he made many trips to the headmaster. So he had a skill.

He lived and worked at 21 Mott Street. He had many children. Among them, my father, Shung, and his sister, Lonnie. Some of his other children were in China. But his wife wasn't allowed to come here because the Chinese Exclusion Act forbid Chinese women to enter the U.S. She was finally able to come much, much later.

I was born here in Chinatown in 1965, and I lived my whole life here, in the same building at 21 Mott Street. I went to P.S. 23, which is now a city-owned building on the corner of Bayard and Mulberry Street. My father went to that same school. But when my father went there, he was the only Chinese kid in the class. It was Italian and Jewish and Irish. By the time I went, there was only one Jewish kid, and the rest were Chinese. And the Jewish kid was the principal's son.

Jan Lee's grandfather, Lee Sing Foon, circa 1890. *Courtesy of June Lee.*

Jan Lee's father, Shung H. Lee, circa 1937. *Courtesy of June Lee.*

Jan Lee on Mott Street in 2012. *Courtesy of Eric Ferrara.*

I had a good friend in the same class named Michael. We'd stop at the seafood store right near my school. And in the morning, women would be buying their fish, frog, turtle, whatever. So Michael and I would stand in front of the window, which was probably up to our chins, and we'd watch the fishmonger hit the fish with a bat and then gut it. For a little seven-year-old kid, it was fascinating.

I used to play in Columbus Park right down here on Mulberry Street. One of the oldest stone pavilions is right here in Columbus Park. It was built in the 1880s. We had some of the best dodge ball games in that building. It's right across the street from P.S. 23. We'd have recess and go play up there. It was much safer than playing outside, where the ball could roll in the street.

When I was a kid living in the building, there were a lot of immigrant families with lots of kids. It was noisier…the energy…the atmosphere. In my father's time, people would leave their doors open because in the summer you'd want the breeze to go through the building. I grew up with a refrigerator, but my father grew up with the Italian ice man who'd carry the block of ice all the way up the stairs and put it in the icebox.

When my father was a kid, the typical tenement apartment had a toilet that sits in a space between the two apartments. And there's two doors—one that opens onto each apartment. So you'd close the doors, do your business and then open the doors. The interesting thing was that when my father was growing up, they were the only Chinese family in the building. An Italian family was next door, and the grandfather from the Italian family didn't speak any English. Now, my grandfather didn't speak any English. But the two men got along fine. And they'd sit in front of the building and drink a scotch every now and then without ever communicating in the same language. But everybody got along well. And I asked my father, "Why…how did all these different cultures get along?" And he said, "It's because everybody was poor." My father often jokes that he had a happy childhood because he didn't know he was poor.

My grandmother, during the Great Depression, had to feed the kids, and they would buy a box of Saltines and a can of condensed milk. And they would have hot water, and they would put condensed milk in the hot water and float a saltine on it, and that's what you had for breakfast.

My father was born here, so of course he spoke English. My dad didn't have any accent whatsoever. My mother came here in 1949. She's Indonesian Chinese. She does have an accent, but she learned English here. And she's always spoken English. By the time I was growing up, there was mostly

English in the household. And the joke in our family was that the parents only spoke Chinese when they didn't want you to understand something.

My mother stayed home, and she cooked for all of us. She's a fantastic cook. My parents were close friends with an Italian family that my father met at work. They'd teach my mother how to cook Italian food, and she'd teach them how to cook Chinese food. So I grew up eating good Italian food. And we had all the traditional Chinese foods at home.

We helped with the chores…all my brothers. We all cook because we watched my mother. We did our shopping all over Chinatown. It was much smaller then. Canal Street was still the borderline between Little Italy and Chinatown. Henry Street was the cutoff to the east. And as far west as Mulberry Street. After Mulberry Street, it was very Italian.

People didn't go to Little Italy that much. Not because of any problem but because there wasn't any real reason to go there, except to go for cappuccino or dessert. After a good meal in Chinatown, we'd go to a café in Little Italy for coffee. And vice versa. People from Little Italy would come here for dinner and go back for their dessert.

Religion? We were raised Taoist. A lot of Chinese raise their children in a combination of Confucian, Taoist and Buddhist beliefs. Most Asian households are Confucian in the sense that the father is the head of the family. The mother handles the finances. Procreation and to have a family and a family name is extremely important. The idea of the afterlife and the many spirits that control the afterlife is really taken from Taoism. Ancestor worship is very deep in my family. In my house, there's a four-foot oil painting of my grandfather with a very elaborate altar.

He died shortly before I was born. He knew in his afterlife his family would feed him nutritionally and spiritually. In the West, if you die, you die. If you don't have any kids, that's that. In Chinese culture, it's very different. Every single holiday we offer our ancestors food and money and offerings and prayers so they are constantly nourished.

When I was a kid, gangs were very bad here in Chinatown. I would never walk on Pell Street and Doyer. My sister Valerie had five kids, and she didn't want her kids to become gang members. So she started the Chinatown Community Youths in 1973. It was at the height of the gang wars. And its purpose was to give the Chinese kids an activity which was the Chinese Lion Dance. This is what you see on the Chinese New Year. You see the big puppet and the big tails. We do that. And we just celebrated our fortieth year. It's totally funded by the family and by donations. And so that became a very important part of my youth.

We were dealing with kids whose parents didn't have two nickels to rub together. But they wanted to protect their kids while they were at a sewing factory, a cook in a restaurant, a delivery guy or a truck driver. We got the kids from working-class families who didn't want their kids to turn bad. Some of them had already turned bad, and they were trying to recover. Some of them were getting beat up because they looked different. Sometimes they were the misfits. Maybe they weren't physically strong. We had Puerto Rican kids, Black kids, Jewish kids. We didn't do anything heroic to save these kids. It was the fact that you belonged to a group that wasn't one of these gangs. It gives children confidence.

I don't think that the era that I lived through was New York at its greatest. And I see New York at a decline—in terms of culture, in originality. When you lived in the era of Warhol, you could go through Greenwich Village area and see all the poets and artists walking around. I think everything now is catch up. It's how do we save that last diner? Or how do we save this last façade? And how do we save the last place this guy sat before he died? Everything is catching up. I think it's too late. The city, instead of lowering taxes, has raised taxes and forced out all the great establishments, whether it's Amato Opera, CBGBs, Max's Kansas City. It forces out the small business owners who are doing something culturally significant.

Chinatown is one of the last bastions because it's here you can still see a continuum from old families...from an older part...an older era of New York that hasn't been completely erased yet. Yet some people—including some Chinese people—want it erased. They want it cleaned up. They say, "It's not looking good for the white people. They'll stop coming."

Nothing could be further from truth. When I was a kid, we had more tourists than we have now. Because of where we are on the island of Manhattan, there's going to be tourism here. And what they're here to see is Chinatown. Not Chinatown filtered through a cliché that looks more like an amusement park or a movie set.

Rebecca Lepkoff

Interviewed in March 2012 at the Lower East Side Tenement Museum during one of Mrs. Lepkoff's photo exhibits

I was born on 60 Hester Street, and the building is still here. My parents were from Russia. I think from the little town of Minsk. They got married, and they came over; my mother was about sixteen, seventeen, and my father was maybe two years older. That must have been 1902.

I was born 1916; my sister Celia was born 1918. Hester Street was very nice. I used to go with my mother shopping on Suffolk Street. There were stores where you buy kosher chicken. And there was a store; on the windows, it was in Yiddish…"Lebedige Fish."

The tradition was you bought the live fish the night before and put it in your bathtub, and the next day, you're supposed to smash it on the head and cut it up. Real gefilte fish is very different than the ones you buy in the jar, you know. You would use the skin and chop up the inside meat and then repack the skin. I used to see my mother with the chopper and the bowl. I don't know who makes it anymore. The good old days!

I'd go, holding my mother's hand. In those days, they never had plastic bags. And they didn't even have paper bags. If you didn't have a carrying bag of your own, they'd just wrap it up in a newspaper.

My family wasn't very religious, but we used to be kosher. And on the holidays we went to the synagogue…it was a few blocks away on Allen Street. There used to be synagogues, two or three on a street. Some of them were very small; some of them were more elaborate. But there were many synagogues.

I can't remember who my neighbors were, but there were a lot of families. There were Polish people, Italian. The Seward Park library wasn't too far

Rebecca Lepkoff in February 2012. *Courtesy of Shell Sheddy.*

from where we lived. After a while we moved. We lived on Clinton Street, Ridge Street and East Broadway. My father would find a better place to live. They started to have bathtubs and bathrooms in the house and steam heat and so on. The bathtub was in the kitchen, underneath that big enamel tray.

I used to play in the Seward Park, and they had a punchball team. You'd play among the other parks…like contests. In my punchball group, there was a Polish girl, an Italian girl, a Jewish girl and an Irish girl. I remember the Irish girl; her name was Margaret Fennesey. And we won the New York City Punchball Team Competition. We were the champions. And we stayed together until we were teens and started to have boyfriends.

In the winter time, we'd go to the Educational Alliance. They had a gym there, so we played basketball. It really was an interracial, international group of playmates.

The Educational Alliance still exists; still on East Broadway. Of course, the population's changed, so now they have a lot of Chinese and Spanish. But back then it was mostly Jewish. And in summer, they had a camp. They had a lot of things free for young children and teenagers.

My father went to night school to learn English. But my mother spoke Yiddish all the time, and that's why I know Yiddish. Right now, my husband—he's a retired teacher from the public school—in the teacher's union, way down on Fulton Street somewhere. They have a Yiddish class, so he goes, and he's learning a lot of Yiddish words. When he comes back, we both practice together because some of the very high adjectives I don't really know.

My father was a workingman, and if he didn't know English, he wouldn't understand if they're giving him the right salary. So all the men workers had to learn English, to know what they're getting was correct. He was a tailor—a very good tailor—and worked for private stores, worked in the garment industry and belonged to the union…Amalgamated Clothing Workers, I think.

We were six kids: three girls and three boys. We used to sleep together, all the girls and the boys. After a while, we had more bedrooms, but we had to share; we learned to share. As a result, we're very easy people to get along with.

My mother made a lot of pot roast, but she could make great chicken soup. And in the summertime she'd make these cold soups called borscht. And the soup made out of sourgrass, called *schav*. You serve cold, with sour cream. And she also made soup out of fruit, out of cherries. A summertime soup. She was a pretty good cook.

The cover of a 1940 Educational Alliance pamphlet advertising a free music event. *Courtesy of the Library of Congress.*

[Number] 343 Cherry Street, where we moved after my husband came back from the war, was an old three-story house. The bathroom was in the hallway. It had a potbelly stove. There was a man that came up and brought coal, and that was in 1945!

And there was no refrigerator; it was an icebox. So, in the summertime, the same man who brought the coal, he'd bring hunks of ice, and you had to put a basin underneath. It was like going back in time, but it was a nice building. I got to know the woman who lived down below. She was very old, but she had two beautiful granddaughters and no man around. I don't know. Mrs. Taylor was her name.

I graduated from Seward Park High School. I became interested in modern dance. I got a scholarship with the Doris Humphrey Company. Then, I auditioned for the World's Fair 1939, and I got a job in *Railroads on Parade*. That was a big show. It had dancers and actors and singers. And it was an Equity show that got paid Equity wages. But I was a Depression kid, so it was the first time I got some real money, outside of my part-time job. So I bought a camera, with my salary, and the first pictures I took were the pushcarts on Suffolk Street and Hester. Also the Third Avenue El, underneath.

The El at Bowery and Houston Streets in 1914. *Courtesy of the Library of Congress.*

So that's how I started photography, but I kept on dancing. I met a well-known photographer; his name was Arnold Eagle, and we became friends. But he also helped me with my photo processing. I set up a darkroom, with chemicals, and bought an enlarger, learned to print. But there was an article in the newspaper *PM* that told about the Photo League, and it spoke about how they were taking photographs on the streets and interested in the real lives of people. And I said, "There's an organization doing this, while I'm just doing it on my own!" So I went down to visit, and I took a class with Sid Grossman, who was a well-known teacher.

The Photo League was on Twenty-first Street and Fourth Avenue—at the bottom of a hotel, I think. They had more than one darkroom, and they had classes and many teachers. And a lot of famous people became interested... Paul Strand. And at that time, it was the McCarthy era. They weren't used to people doing documentary work. "Documentary? They must be Communists!" So they cautioned us. Are we Communists or...something?

Eventually they sent an FBI agent who posed as a student, and she reported that one of the teachers would talk about Communists. They put us on the list of Communists Red, posted our organization in the newspapers. So the place just closed up because people were scared to be affiliated. If you were affiliated, you'd also be put on the list, and nobody would hire you. Nobody. So that was the end of the Photo League.

I'm in my nineties...I can't lie about it. But these photographs that I have on the wall, they are very well loved. I always thought that life on the street was full of action. And even to this very day, you go out in the street; it's like a theater, and everything is happening. People doing this and that.

At that time, I really liked my neighborhood. I liked the Jewish people. People would come out in the street and socialize; their apartments were small, whatever. They'd come out and hang out in the grocery store...or sit on the stoop. If you had a baby, you'd go out with the baby carriage. And I thought, "That's such an interesting life!"

And also, when I was a dancer, I studied choreography. And on stage, which is like an eight-by-ten photograph, this person sits here and...so I had a good instinct on how something should sit on a photograph.

At 343 Cherry Street, there was an extra room, and that was the darkroom. But later on I didn't have a room, I'd print at night. I'd have the enlarger in the kitchen or somewhere I could pull the shades down. Because I was pretty peppy, and I used to print through the night...as soon as it got dark.

I had three children, and I have four grandchildren. I managed. Well, I say, if you have a passion, you'll do it. Your passion will push you to do what you want to do. It's your passion that will create very good work.

I met my husband at a dance class…he could dance, but he ended up as a teacher. After my first son was born, we moved to Knickerbocker Village. It's down near Madison and Catherine, toward Chinatown, where the Third Avenue El used to be. The El was a wonderful way of going up to Fourteenth Street and Forty-second Street.

I raised my children. I tried to be a good mother, and I did my photography. The war years were very hard. My husband and my brothers were in the war…you prayed that nothing would happen to them.

I worked at a photo studio, on Forty-second Street and Fifth, the Pavell Photo Finishing Studio, and I worked at private studios. Photography…it was easy to get a job. All the men were away at the war, so there were jobs…all over.

Going back to the Photo League…in the '40s there were very few people with cameras in the first place, so if I was taking a photo on the street, somebody would come over and say, "So, what's that, your boyfriend?" At that time, there weren't any photographers taking life as it is; they were taking commercial photography, portrait photography and fashion. The Photo League was the first organization that opened up the idea to take photographs…of life, how it is, life on the streets…People, how they live…how they work…how they look. They introduced an aspect of seeing that didn't exist. They were functioning very well and being recognized by a lot of prestigious people, until they folded up in '51.

And I wonder, if they didn't fold, how would they have developed, into what…because they were so passionate and so avant-garde…about photography.

Anna De Robertis Mansueto

Interviewed October 2002 at Mrs. Mansueto's family pastry shop, De Robertis Pasticeria, 176 First Avenue

My grandfather came from a town on the Adriatic, and he started the business here. It's been here since 1904. They came here to change their life, and they did…change their life around. Originally it was called Pugliese's Café, and my father changed it over to De Robertis Pastry Shop.

My mother's family came from Naples. The same reason. Try to make a better life, and they did. I think they did a fantastic job…for people who did not have an education. Especially my father, who went up to the third grade. Built this business and took care of this business, and he didn't have a college education. You don't need a college education. A lot of it is common sense and being nice to the people all the time; it means a lot. And he used to always tell me as a little girl growing up, "It's not the quantity of people that come to the door, it's the quality that you put out and that brings everybody back."

And you know what? He was right. I miss him. I wish he was here, but he's not. But I know he's here. His soul is walking around. His spirit is here; it didn't leave. That I'm convinced of.

What was it like growing up around here? We have the building; the place is ours.

We lived right upstairs. There was never any problems. There was no gates. The hallways weren't locked. Everybody would watch out for everybody's children. You did something wrong…"Ah, what do you think you're doing!?" We wouldn't dare go tell our mothers on Mrs. So and So hollering at us because we'd get the rest of it.

Anna Mansueto and brother John De Robertis at their café in 2012. *Courtesy of Eric Ferrara.*

Anna and John outside De Robertis Café in 2012. *Courtesy of Eric Ferrara.*

Our building is a walk-up. I grew up with electricity. I grew up with full bathrooms. This is what we had here. The building is old, it's not that it's new. It's over a hundred years old. But you see electric was here, bathrooms were here.

The stores have changed. There were a lot of different stores. There used to be a drugstore up at the corner. Then there was a pasta store. That's all they made was just pasta, nothing else. Lanza's Restaurant was there. That was my other grandfather. My mother's father started Lanza's. I know more my father's family. And then there was a pizzeria down here, down the steps. My uncle had that. That store has changed. It was a nut store, then it was a small furniture store. There's a lot of big changes. The whole neighborhood has changed.

This area was a very mixed area. It had Jewish, it had Italians. You had Polish, Germans, Russians, Ukrainians. We really got along with everybody else. Even if you didn't understand them, your hands were your language. After a while, you understood each other, and they start learning the English language. It was a lot of fun, and you learned about different cultures. And I see the whole neighborhood turning around again the way it was. You got different cultures coming in, which is very interesting. To try to appreciate somebody else's culture because it's nice.

Socialize? What did we do? Let's see. Ah, my father was a little bit on the strict side, so I didn't get out that often. I went to church dances. I went to Mary Help of Christians on Twelfth Street; that's where I got baptized. Communion, Confirmation, got married there.

On Sunday, I went to church; we had to go to church. I stayed here with my father in the store. It was busy during the day; people coming out of church. The women come out of church, and then they'd go home and start cooking. My mother did the cooking, so everybody was always upstairs by her. My grandmother used to do all the cooking. I swear I look at my house, and I've become my grandmother. Now I do all the cooking.

My dreams? My dreams were…to get married. Have a family, go out to work, have a nice house. And I have all that. I work hard to keep what I have, and I appreciate everything I have. I appreciate what my father left me, and I appreciate the building…the house that I have. It doesn't come out of thin air any of this stuff; you work hard, appreciate what you have, and when you do it shows. It shows in the house, it shows in the business, it shows in everything. It shows in my staff. I got a great staff; they are. They're great.

Growing up around here, we had fun. Games outside? We'd put the chalk and play hopscotch. We weren't…I wasn't allowed to go too far. I had to

The entrance of Mary Help of Christians on East Twelfth Street in 2012. *Courtesy of Eric Ferrara.*

stay between Eleventh Street and Tenth Street. All the girls, the same thing. None of the girls were allowed off the block; we had to stay put. We made our own games up.

My father knew what time I went to school and what time I'd be home. As I got older and I started dating my husband—he's the only one I went out with—I had to be home at twelve o'clock. We'd get home around eleven thirty, and my father'd be standing in front of the door checking his watch. That's how he was. Nobody believes it.

Up to now, I've had a good life. It's had its ups and downs, but I always say God gives you what you can only shoulder. I feel like I shoulder a lot, but if I couldn't carry it, he wouldn't make me do it. What the future holds for me…I don't know. I just say let me be good. Let everybody be healthy around me. Because if you're not healthy, money and everything means nothing.

I got four children. Two are married, two are single. I can't ask for anything else. I got good memories growing up here. I just hope the store stays another hundred years in the family, but nobody knows. I'm going to say the same thing my father said…it's here for them. If they want it. It's long hours, it's hard work. If they don't want it, then they do what they have to do. I feel the same way. I cannot push it on them. Me? I always wanted to go downstairs and learn how to do the baking. My father said, "No, that's for the boys. You're up here with me." And I still would love to know how to decorate a cake.

ANNA MILETICH

*Interviewed in August 2005 at St. Stanislaus Church
on East Seventh Street*

My family came from Poland, and they settled in Pennsylvania because of the coal mines. My father worked in the coal mines. I come from a large family; my mother had twelve children. And out of the twelve, I'm the only one left now. Isn't that something?

We had a rough life. My mother had to take care of the family, so everyone had to do their share of work. We had a little farm, so we had to go before the sun came up. We had to go pick tomatoes before they got overripe. Then we came home, and my mother made breakfast. And then we went to school.

I came to New York because there was no work there. The silk mills didn't take me because you had to have some kind of experience. That was in the '30s, during the Depression.

My husband was born on the East Side. He was born on Seventh Street and Avenue B. I first came to New York about 1933. They had trolleys and horses and wagons. I met my husband here. He's Polish, so we met at a Polish dance picnic. Then they had a hall on St. Mark's Place, the Polish National Home. That later became the Electric Circus. And all the young girls, we used to go dancing there.

In 1935, I got married. When I got married, I was doing housework, and I was working for very nice Jewish people. They gave me clothes to get married and everything. I lived on the West Side, on Twenty-first Street and Eighth Avenue. And then I became pregnant, and I had my son. We moved to St. Marks Place between Second and Third Avenues around 1938. I lived in that same building for forty-five years or so. It was number 32; a very famous building. And it was a very famous block. It was homey. Then it turned to be hippies, beatniks, flower children. Back then, it was nice Polish people. The neighbors were there a long time.

We bought a little business there—a grocery store in the building. That was in the middle '50s. My son went to school in P.S. 64, the school on Ninth Street. Then he went to Seward Park. After he graduated from Seward Park, he went to the service in Korea.

I went to church at St. Georges on Seventh Street and Third Avenue. I used to come to this church, too. I have two boys. One got baptized at Mary Help of Christians on Twelfth Street. And then he made his Communion in Nativity.

I worked because my husband...at that time war broke out. You remember the '40s.

And my husband went to work in the Navy Yards...in Brooklyn. And I used to do housework for this Jewish woman. I took my son with me to clean the house. And she was so sweet to me, that woman. And if I worked a little later, her chauffeur would bring me home. And she'd give me food. Very nice people. They lived on Eighty-sixth Street and Fifth Avenue. And when she wanted me, the chauffeur would come pick me up.

The subway was five cents. I'd take the subway at Cooper Union; take it to Forty-second Street. The shuttle was free. Then I'd take the Seventh Avenue train up to 160th Street. She moved up to 160th, so I went there. The subway was underground, but they had a Third Avenue El, a Second Avenue El. They had a Sixth Avenue El, a Ninth Avenue El.

Movies? We used to go. Years ago there was an Orpheum; now it's *Stomp* there. And then there was St. Marks Movies on Second Avenue and St. Marks. I think there was something on Avenue B. We used to go to Loews on Second Avenue. Then it became the Village East...no...the Fillmore East. See, the mind don't function no more when you get a certain age.

On Sunday, we used to go to Central Park, Battery Park; we did a lot of walking. Took the kids out. Tompkins Park was right here. My mother-in-law lived on 149 Avenue A. We'd make sandwiches, and we sat in Tompkins Square Park. They had a swimming pool there. It was beautiful...all families...kids. That park also changed a lot. Like every six years, the whole area changes. Now this is considered the Village.

I told you, we had a grocery store on St. Marks Place. We didn't sell it. No, we had to close it up. Couldn't sell it. And we opened up a bar and restaurant...an artist's bar...in the Village on University Place. Dylan's Bar.

The century-old Temperance Fountain of Tompkins Square Park. *Courtesy of Nina Howes.*

That was, I think, 1959. It was on University and Eleventh Street. Artists and teachers from NYU came in there. We met many actors and writers: Arthur Miller, Veronica Lake. Barbara Streisand came in; she was young. And many jazz musicians came in.

It was a very lively place. Mingus...and the guy who wrote "Take Five," and many stars I don't remember. And the artist Frances Klein, and a lot of abstract artists...De Kooning. De Kooning gave my son a painting. They were drunk, and my son was young. And at that time they were all broke. But that place we had to give up. They wanted too much rent. We couldn't afford it. And from there we bought a store uptown—Sixty-fourth Street and Third Avenue. Benny Goodman lived near there. The Rockefellers used to come in...Jayne Mansfield. We met a lot of people...wonderful people.

Being on the Lower East Side didn't change me in any way because my kids...now today...they have condos in Florida. And they want me to go. Being that I'm older, they don't want me to be alone here. But I don't want to live in Florida. No. This is my place. I love people. I like excitement. I like action. I don't want to be with the birds and the squirrels. That's not for me. I can't sit on a rocking chair.

I had a very full life, an exciting life. It's my son's anniversary today. So we'll be going out to dinner. And all my kids got married. The oldest one, he's sixty-eight. He has three children, and those three children got children, so I have six great-grandchildren. So I'm up there. What can I say?

JOHN MILISENDA

Interviewed in January 2012 at Theater for the New City on Second Avenue and East Tenth Street

My grandfather came from Sicily, from a small town, Racalmuto. After five years, he sent for his wife and his daughter, Mary. When they came to Ellis Island, they were pulled off the line because Mary had an eye infection. My grandmother covered Mary up so the doctor couldn't see her eyes, and they moved right through. They lived on Chrystie Street in two rooms. My dad was the youngest of five kids; he was born in 1919. All the kids slept in one bed.

They took showers once a week at a place on Allen Street. It cost them about a nickel. When my dad moved to 72 East Third Street, there was a bathtub in the kitchen. He thought he'd moved into a hotel. During the Depression, things were tough, but there was always food on the table. [Number] 72 East Third Street was full with the Milisenda family and the Charelli family, which were my uncles. My grandmother cooked for all of them.

I was born in October 1947. We lived at 252 East Houston Street, between Avenue A and B. There was a scrap metal yard just up the street, with a corrugated metal fence and a giant magnet on a steam shovel that used to pick up metal all day long. You could hear it. And right next to 252, they sold Jewish monuments—stones, gravestones. There was also a building that looked like a flatiron building on Houston Street right off of Avenue A.

I lived on the ground floor at 252 East Houston. I think the bathroom was in the hallway, and the bathtub was in the kitchen. We had an icebox because I remember the man screaming out, "Yo ice!" when I was a kid,

John Milisenda and his mom, Rose, on East Third Street in 2012. *Courtesy of Eric Ferrara.*

and then we moved up to a refrigerator. My dad was one of the first in the neighborhood, in the early '50s, to buy a television set. So most of our neighbors were in our house looking at TV.

He was a very creative guy, my father. He painted. He played guitar. He had a high school education, but he was an extremely curious man. He was a member of the Hayden Planetarium. He built a telescope with a six-inch mirror and the tubes that linoleum came with in those days. We'd go on the roof and look at the moon.

I went to local public schools. I started out at P.S. 63 on Third Street. Then I attended a school on Norfolk Street...between Rivington and Delancey. I went to Straubenmuller Junior High School 22. That was on Columbia Street off of Houston. After that I went to Seward Park High School on Essex Street and Grand. Tony Curtis went there; so did Walter Matthau, and so did I! Some guys told me Walter Matthau sold socks and ties on First Street in front of Pop's candy store before his career took off as an actor.

First Street...we were a "play street." There was a sign that said, "Play Street. Deliveries can be made to businesses only." We could play stickball, whatever. We had the street to ourselves; we didn't have to worry about traffic. We played Ring-O-Levio—that was a game of tag. And you run into your opponent, and you hold onto them and you say, "Ring-O-levio, one, two, three; one, two, three." And if they can't escape you, they go into a dungeon. And then you collect the other team, and when the whole team's collected, you go out.

We played Skellzies. It was a game with thirteen boxes chalked onto the street. And you'd have bottle caps, and you had to go through thirteen boxes. And then you'd become a killer to knock your opponents out. The more opponents you killed before they killed you, you'd win. It was a game of elimination. We also played hide-and-seek.

Against the wall of the Cristadora House on First Street, people would pitch pennies. And the people that got the pennies closest to the edge of the building won the game. We played a game called Off the Tip, and that's stoopball. There's a cornice at the bottom of the building. And we'd have these pink balls, and you'd bounce it against the cornice. And there'd be a line of kids, and if they caught the ball you'd be out. But if they dropped it, or if it bounced, each bounce was a base. One bounce was first base. Two bounces was second base. You'd hit a home run when you had four bounces. But there was always disputes about if the ball was in bounds or out of bounds. We argued more than we played; it was too much fun.

In the summertime, we'd play in the backyards behind 88 East First Street. It was smelly. People would throw garbage there. And the janitors would chase us out. We'd go back anyway. And on a hot summer night, we'd play on the roofs. We'd be playing Ring-O-Levio. And we'd be running around and around, and then all of a sudden the kids would be tearing from one roof to the other. And this old lady with a broom, Mrs. Topenycky, would come out and say, "Bums! Go where you live!" And she'd chase us. Luckily no one ran off the roof.

On the Fourth of July, there were fireworks all over the Lower East Side. And three weeks before July 4…Boom. Boom. Boom! Kids would be setting off fireworks. You could buy a pack of firecrackers…twenty in a pack…for ten cents.

We had seasons. Scooter season's where you'd take your old broken roller skates, pull the wheels off, get a two-by-four from the lumberyard. For ten cents you got a pound of nails. We'd chip in for everything. Somebody would have two cents, three cents. And everybody'd share nails. Get a wooden milk crate and nail it down. Put two handles on it and scoot up and down the block. My uncle Charley bought me my first tricycle on Avenue A. And I was the most popular kid on the block. Everyone wanted to take turns riding it.

My father, Salvatore, was a barber. His shop was at 80 East First Street between Avenue A and First Avenue. In the middle of the building there was a staircase; on the left side was a Chinese hand laundry. On the right side was my dad's barbershop. And in the winter of February 1957, I came out, and there were two Chinese boys throwing a ball to each other; they were about my age. And I asked them to throw the ball to me. And the younger brother said to the older brother, "Mo," which means "no." And the older brother threw it to me anyway, and we became the best of friends.

His grandfather, Lum Lee, would cook Chinese food and share it with my dad. Leonard and I went to the Boys Club together on Tenth Street and Avenue A. There was lots of settlement houses. The Boys Brotherhood Republic was on Second Street, I think, between Avenue B and C. I went to the Cristadora House when it was on First Street.

There were derelicts all over the Bowery. Most of them were World War II veterans that were shellshocked and fell between the cracks. My dad had a very kind heart; he'd invite them into his barbershop and feed them. They never bothered me as a child. I was never afraid of them. They'd get into fistfights with one another. You'd see puddles of blood on the streets sometimes.

My mother was Jewish—from Ekaterinoslav in the Ukraine. My parents met on East Third Street 'cause they lived right across the street from each other. And they'd sneak out on dates 'cause it was taboo for a Jewish woman to date a Christian man. They went to Nativity Church on Second Avenue and met with a priest, and the priest told my father you're going to go to hell if you marry her. So they eloped. Her parents didn't speak to her for a year for marrying a Christian.

My mother was a mom at home. Each day she'd go shopping at the Safeway on Avenue A, between Second and Third Street. There were bakeries everywhere. Italian bakeries. You could smell the scent of fresh bread every night. When I woke up in the morning, the whole neighborhood smelled like bread.

Between Orchard and Ludlow…that used to be Henry's Delicatessen and right next to it…that was Craig's. They had the most incredible pastries you ever tasted. They made a chocolate ganâche cake. It wasn't gourmet or anything like that. It was cake for everybody. And on Essex Street, there was a place called Morris's, between Rivington and Stanton. He had bialys with more onions on it than you could imagine. And he'd open up this cube of butter with a wooden paddle, and you'd chunk it off.

John Milisenda standing in a Cub Scout uniform, with his friend Leonard Lum to his left and mom, Rose (seated), 80 East First Street, June 8, 1957. *Courtesy of John Milisenda.*

93

Number 80 East First Street on January 3, 1965, three years before the building was razed. *Courtesy of John Milisenda.*

On Rivington, there was an old-fashioned grocery store, which had giant burlap bags full of beans, peas. You could scoop it out—pistachio nuts, or beans or dried fruits. Now it's a fancy restaurant.

The neighborhood…there was Polish, Ukrainian, Italian, Jewish, some Puerto Rican. There were neighborhoods you couldn't walk through because the violence was so bad, like on Forsyth Street. Every week there were shootouts. In the early '60s, heroin hit Forsyth Street, then it hit alphabet city.

Once, I'm on Rivington Street, and this nurse is standing there—in this doctor's office—blood running all over her. It turns out a drug addict went in there looking for heroin for a fix. And the nurse didn't have it…So he stabbed her, and she's standing there bleeding. So it was heroin that was really bad news.

I never got into that. I was too excited about photography. What inspired me? My dad. He'd take photographic film and develop it. We'd do this in the bathroom. We put a blanket up over the window, and my mother would complain nobody could get in there. And we put a folding table over the bathtub and processed film running water from the bathtub.

And I met a photography instructor, Arthur Freed, at the Educational Alliance on East Broadway. He taught me photography in a way I couldn't even imagine. I was always documenting the neighborhood. I started taking photographs, probably in '59. I read a lot of technical magazines. I took them out from the library on East Broadway, by a little city park. I used to go there all the time.

I photographed that neighborhood, and I'm so grateful that I did 'cause I go back there now and there's nothing of it left. Everything...is totally gone.

TARA MOHAMMED

*Interviewed in November 2002 at a coffee shop on
Nineteenth Street and First Avenue*

I grew up on Eldridge Street, number 202. That building does not exist today. What was interesting about those houses, we had an icebox. So the man came around every day saying, "Iceman! Iceman!" We bought the ice and put it in the box. We didn't have a regular stove. So the man came around every day and said, "Coal! Coal!" So we bought the coal and put it in the oven to cook our food. And the bathtub was in the kitchen. The bathroom was in the hall.

I was there in the '50s. In fact, when I graduated from Seward Park High School...You know Bernard Schwartz? He graduated from Seward Park High School also. You know who Bernard Schwartz is? Tony Curtis! He graduated four years before me.

He used to live in the Lower East Side. The teachers told him to follow his heart. And as soon as he married Janet Leigh, he brought her back to Seward Park to show his teachers who he married.

My family was from India. My father was a doctor. He came here; I don't know why. And we grew up here. We were really happy. Everybody from every place lived in that same building. The Italians...the feast of San Gennaro would have the festival in the middle of every year. They would carry the statue on their shoulders. And people used to throw money on the statue. We had Jews, Christians and Muslims living in the same house. And we were all friends. People in the summertime used to sleep on their fire escapes because you weren't afraid of anybody. We all looked out for each other. I don't remember where my father worked, and my mother was a mother and a housewife.

Seward Park High School at the corner of Grand and Ludlow Streets in 2012. *Courtesy of Eric Ferrara.*

Shopping? That's going to make you laugh. At that time on the Lower East Side, they didn't have an Indian area. But since we lived on Eldridge Street we used to shop in Chinatown. Why? Because my father could speak Cantonese. Before he came here, he was in Singapore. We went shopping in Chinatown and got everything we needed.

When I was little, I went to school right across from that synagogue on Eldridge Street between Hestor and Canal. That was junior high school, P.S. 65, Charles Sumner. Today, that school is called the Chinese International Junior High.

One of the national languages in India is English because we were under the British at one time. And each part of India—each state—speaks their own language. For example, in Calcutta we speak Bengali but also English and Hindustani.

We spoke English all the time. In fact, I tell people now, "Don't lose your language. If you come to this country, teach your children your language. Because when you lose your language, you start losing your culture."

We learned to read and write when we were at home. My mother taught us. So what happened was when we went to school, I was skipped up two years. That's our culture, your mother teaches you.

On the weekends, we were family oriented. That's very Indian. So you have your friends or family visiting New York. Even if you have a small tiny room, you didn't put people in a hotel. They all stayed there with you. And my father took us every place because he had a car.

We saw ice skating. We saw Coney Island. We went to the museum. I did go to the mosque. They didn't have many; they just had one in Brooklyn. We used to go just on holidays to pray. And we'd pray at home. And on holidays with my Christian friends, I'd do Christmas carols. And on the High Holy days of the Jewish Holy Days, I'd go with them too because we're friends. I'm Muslim, but we're taught we all came from the same Creator. And we're all going to be judged by our behavior here. So you have to share and take care of others and live and love in harmony. And that's all written in the Koran.

After high school, I got married, and all my friends went off to college. But when I wasn't married anymore, that's when I went back to college to get my education. So I said I'm going to help humanity in every way I can.

Rock and roll...I was a Beatles fan. The Beatles came in the '60s. We listened to all kinds of music—classical music, Indian music. And we went to the University Settlement on Eldridge and Rivington Street, and they had recreational programs for children. And in the summertime, they sent you off to Beacon, New York, to a camp. I don't know if they have any of that any more.

My father had a lot of friends. And on the weekends, people would come. And they'd bring out the Indian instruments, and they'd play music at our house, and everybody would jump up and dance. We had a great time. I'm so thankful to God for growing up on Eldridge Street. And even Rabbi Swiss now...everybody knows I'm Muslim when I go to that shul, but they all know me as his sister from Eldridge Street. I'm sixty-five, and he's eighty-three, and he tells me I'm one of the last people alive that he knows that lived on Eldridge Street. Many of them that I know, they've gone or passed away. The others moved to Florida. So now when we hold our Seward Park High School reunion, they have it in Florida at the same time.

The Lower East Side was a happy place for everybody all over the world. That's why I believe in what our religion teaches us: that we must share. I'm going to keep giving back, sharing with everybody I can. I'm a teacher. I'm a nurse. I'm a Middle Eastern dancer and have traveled all over the world. Every time I opened up my mouth, they said, "Oh, you're from New York." I said, "How do you know?" They said, "You've got a New York accent." I said I didn't know I even had an accent.

Tom O'Hara

Interviewed in February 2012 at Nom Wah Tea Parlor on Doyers Street

I was born in 1929—two and a half months before the Crash—in my grandfather's house in Brooklyn. My grandfather was a hatter, originally from Ireland. And my mother was born in Sicily. My father just started working for Swift and Company. The Depression hit, and luckily he didn't lose his job. Things got really tough…very much like today. Then my mother got a good job at C.O. Miller's Department Store as a corset buyer, so we moved up there, to Connecticut.

I lived there until I went to the navy. When the war ended, I was sixteen. With these eyes, I got to see Evita Peron. I was really surprised. Buenos Aires was quite a sight.

I'm a history buff, and the people I found the most fascinating were the Chinese. I was living at the McBurney YMCA on Twenty-third Street. And I said, "Chinatown! Here's a good chance to learn something!" And I came down here.

There were lots of Italians who came here to shop and eat, and there were always people that came to Chinatown 'cause it was a place to see. But I was different. I began asking questions, and Chinese people began to be fascinated with *me*. Here's a guy who doesn't ask dumb questions, and the next thing you know, I had two or three friends. And then I met a guy, Tip Eng, who was born in Kwang Tung China and came here when he was six.

I was invited to dances, parties, friends' houses. I got invited to join a Chinese club, and they named it Say Hoy…the Four Seas Association. The Chinese believe in a world—a North Sea, a West Sea, an East Sea and a

Tom O'Hara on Mott Street in 2012. *Courtesy of Eric Ferrara.*

South Sea. That's from ancient times. And when they say, *"Say-Hoy, Chin – Noy,* inside the Four Seas," it means "All of humanity, all men are brothers."

Chinatown was smaller then. This is Chinatown, right here! Doyers Street, Pell Street, most of Mott Street from Canal south…till the end of the street. And that was Chinatown. And Mosco Street, which was then called Park Row. Mulberry Street was supposed to be Italian, but even when I was here, there were a couple of funeral homes that were already Chinese.

Between the Italians and the Chinese, they mostly ignored one another. And then there were those personal relationships that happen everywhere. There were some Italians who realized Italy is one of the oldest cultures in Europe, and China's the oldest culture in Asia. You know, we have something in common.

And I'd say that the majority of the Christian Chinese belong to the Lutheran Church, because *it was here*! Right? There was the True Light Lutheran Church down on Mott Street, and they had a school. So a lot of the Chinese kids went to the school. The parents remained Buddhist or Tao. But hey!

It was 1953. I was living in the Y. And then my sister, she broke up with her husband, and somebody got us a place to live on Pell Street. Number 12 Pell Street. Me and my sister, we lived up on the fourth floor, right in the heart of Chinatown. We made breakfast cereal; the usual western breakfast. But lunch we bought Chinese. We bought, or I began to learn how to cook.

Pell Street was a totally Chinese street even then. See, unlike Mott Street, the corner…I still joke about it 'cause now it's a Chinese place. The northeast corner of Orchard Street and Mott was the only Italian-owned place on Mott Street. I think there might have been one or two other places. Mott Street from Canal down to the Bowery was exclusively Chinese.

Orchard Street was mostly Chinese; farther west you went, the more Italian it became. Pell Street was totally Chinese. And that was it. Curio shops, coffee shops. By the way, that's a big joke. I thought the Chinese only drank tea. I worked in a coffee shop that's now a restaurant, right across the street from the church. It was Lonnie's Coffee Shop. And the Chinese, I found, were the biggest coffee drinkers in the world! I'm thinking, "It must be the Irish drinkin' all the tea!"

Lonnie was born here. She spoke Cantonese fluently, but she wanted an open shop. They had a jukebox in there, mostly popular music—Bing Crosby. We made sandwiches…tuna fish. It was not a "Chinese restaurant" in that sense.

Inside a Chinese grocery store in 1942. *Courtesy of the Library of Congress.*

In Chinese, the bamboo, it's hollow or it's not. And *jookok*—the strong bamboo—that would mean people who are familiar with Chinese ways. They did things the old-fashioned way. You'd hear this going on in Cantonese and English all the time. *Took-san*, the empty bamboo, the American-born that don't know anything. That was an insult!

There was a place right at the end of Pell Street, crossover was 39 Mott Street—Sam Wo, "Three United." The main waiter was kinda' gutsy...always wore a white apron. I'd walk in there, "Hey, Lo-fan!" Instead of regular Cantonese, he'd use the village dialect. A lot of the people around here came from that district, and I'd hear people say, "Oh, no, that's four district dialect!" Wow, people puttin' each other down for their dialect, for their sub-dialects.

With the Four Seas Association, we used to throw dances all the time. Right here in the Four Seas Association Building. I was the house manager. I lived upstairs, 22 Pell Street. And I took care of the second floor. We had music… played records. 1959. A little rock…something you could get romantic about. Till two in the morning. Pell Street was a jumpin' street. There was a bar down the end, toward Mott. It was called Golden Dragon. We'd go in there on weekends and drink till two, three in the morning. It's a restaurant now. Pell Street had a lot of great places, noodle shops.

And then there was Doyers Street. This was the esoteric part of Chinatown. There was a terrible place…Eurasia…East/West…and boy, there's the place that had the fights. When you went by the door, you looked to see that nothing was moving toward you. I think they sold Chinese pastries, but nobody did any *cooking*. It was a big bar and full of prostitutes. There were a lot of Lo-fan going in there, looking for action.

Then I got married, and we came back here a lot. Every Tuesday, I come down here. We meet at the Jing Fong, on Elizabeth Street. People know who we are. We catch up with each other.

CARMEN PABON

*Interviewed in February 2001 at her apartment on
East Fifth Street and Avenue D*

I came from Puerto Rico in 1946, on March 23. It was so cold I cried. I say I'm not going to stay here; it's too much for me. I miss the hot weather. But I have to stay because the situation in Puerto Rico was so bad. I came to 116th to buy a coat. I never forget that coat. Oh, that color.

About a week after I came, I was looking for a job, and the neighbor of my friend said, "Go across the street. They need people to work sewing baby clothes and cleaning the clothes and packing." And I went. Eight in the morning the man says to me, "You could stay 'cause we need to pack all these clothes. You want to work as a floor lady?" I said I don't care. I need the job.

In '48, I went back to Puerto Rico. I stay a couple of months, and I come back again because the situation very bad. My mother raised three of us, and what we eat was fruit from the country. And we went to the farm, and we work for twelve cents a day—picking peppers and tomatoes and beans. And then I found another job doing tobacco factory. And I cry so much because my intention was to finish school.

I went to school only to seventh grade. But I was very bright and smart. When I came to this country, I didn't need to worry about speaking English because I learn in Puerto Rico. I had a good teacher that was Puerto Rican, but she was raised in this country, and with her I learned the English.

I went to San Juan to work, to stay in my cousin's house, and I worked in a clinic that they help the womans, the prostitution womans. In 1942, when all the marines went to Puerto Rico.

Carmen Pabon on East Fifth Street in 2012. *Courtesy of Nina Howes.*

Then I met a man. I was talking to him, and he pay me the trip to come here. I don't got the money. He died with TB. At that time, everybody was sick in Puerto Rico with TB. They don't have enough food to eat and suffering so much.

My second husband, he left me in '71. I go through pain with him because he was drinking, using drugs. I raised this family myself. I was going every day to school. There were seven kids. "Ma, what you need?" When I get sick in the hospital, all of them were there. And the doctor say, "What is this?" I say, "My family, they came for me. I'm a mother. I raised them alone."

After they all leave from me, I get involved in the community. I get involved with Charas. Because in Puerto Rico, even when I was younger…fourteen, fifteen…I make campaign in the country. I remember they put a cart, and they make for the people to come and vote.

They give coffee and bread and food. Ooooh…they buy your vote. Now I'm involved in everything—every meeting, community board, police meeting. I know all the way to go to downtown to the different office. That's why in the community everybody know me because I help the people. I help in the garden for almost three years; treating the homeless in there. I bring the people to the meetings. I knew all the priests that came to St. Brigid's in fifty years. I used to pick up all the kids from the school to take them to the classes for the First Communion, with Sister Magdalena. Always the churches were helping people; poor people that need food. The Catholic Charities. I used to take people over there that need help.

What I liked most is that I get so involved in the meetings of the community board. In the fight, the struggle.

I get this apartment. I'm here since December 5, 1950. You know how much I pay? Thirty-six dollar a month. For five rooms. They tried to take me out from this apartment. But I have a lot of good connections. That's why I involved in the community. Because it's the only way you could have somebody to help you. And to fight. And I used to leave seven o'clock from this house to take somebody to the welfare, to the social security, to the court, up to Harlem.

That's why they put my name the "Mother Teresa of the Lower East Side." I say I'm not "Mother Teresa of the Lower East Side," I'm Carmen Pabon from the Lower East Side. A lot of ladies say, "Why? Why you feeding that people?" I say that people could be you. And I was picking clothes from everybody that donate to me, and I was dressing the people in the street.

My daughter says, "Mom we got to buy a beeper for you, because we call and we never find you." And I say, "Uh uh. I don't want no beeper." *Pata*

St. Brigid's Church on Avenue B. *Courtesy of Nina Howes.*

Caliente comes when she feels like coming. But you know something? I help the people. And they say how much is going to charge me to help me go to welfare. I say, "Charge you? Let's go." If they don't have the money for carfare, we walk.

In the '50s, the people in the church, all of them work together. A lot of Puerto Rican people used to live in this neighborhood with the Jewish. The problem with drug come to the neighborhood in '65. The Jewish people that had the stores on Avenue C, they move out from the neighborhood. There were so much drugs.

I remember when they burned the stores to the Jewish. There was a riot, and they burned all those stores on Avenue C. When I came to this apartment, there was a few Jewish people living. Then they started leaving.

When I came to the Lower East Side was not that bad. Everybody was very together and respect each other. You don't hear about girl in the street with a kid. The language they have now.

The schools were good; you don't have to fear anything happen to the kids. But now they gotta lock their doors like a jail. So many things happening. Right now they clean a lot of the drug around here, but it's hiding. It's there. It's not like before, but it's there. Tompkins Park in the '50s was clean. Was no drugs. After '65, the drugs coming.

You see the people injecting; some people die in the street…I didn't have that problem with my kids. On Friday night, they say, "Mom, we're going to a dance." They get together, fifteen…fourteen…they go in a group…they come back in a group. And they give me the phone number where they are going.

We used to fight a lot for the buildings when they started taking the people out from the apartments. Fire, everything. That was a mess from '65 to '80; fight, guns, everything. Killing so many young kids.

My dreams were to raise my family and give all the support I could, and for me, I'm so happy. I was ambitious to be a nurse. My mother can't afford it. I was very smart in school. They say, "You are so smart ma'am; you could finish the high school." And I say, "Yeah. My experience is the University of the Street…with the people."

And I'm a social worker from the Lord, with no graduation, no paper in my hand. I'm here fifty years on the Lower East Side. For me, it's like being in Puerto Rico. Because I get along with everybody.

You know what, I see the change in this community. I don't blame the people that came from the outside. I blame few political people that were involved. That's why gentrification…it's terrible. Now where the people is going to go? Because they raise the rent. Now the welfare don't help you.

What you going to do with $300 when the landlords are raising the rent. Some people sold the apartment to the speculators…condos…"condoms."

Before, when the drug was here, they didn't come. They didn't care about the ghetto, the Lower East Side, but now that it's clean. Then the gentrification started, and all these white people coming down here.

Now who's going to go to jail? No more Puerto Rican; no more blacks. Who's going to go? All the *Blanquitos* that come on Friday to spend the nights drinking in those bars? Only you see now is bars…everywhere. You see Avenue D?

Living on the Lower East Side…I see the change in the community. And I see that our people and the black people, they're not going to have a place to live. What they want is to take the people, the poor people, out from the neighborhood, that the rich people come in.

But I said to myself, they can't move me out. I never been late in the rent, never had a complaint. I'm grateful to God because I was raised so poor that sometime we have to take the leaf of orange to boil it and drink to go to bed. We used to go to the river to get fishes at night, and we come about five thirty in the morning and cook it, every day.

I have to give something from this house to a person every day. The day I don't do it, I feel that I didn't do nothing worthy. I told my children like that—defend the Puerto Rican culture. Most of these kids…their parents don't tell them the story. How you do for your family to be what they are today.

What the people don't think about is God give us this land to cultivate—the best piece of cake. God is showing us, little by little, we need to care.

Joe Preston

Interviewed in January 2012 at Mr. Preston's apartment on East Eleventh Street

My great-grandmother came here from Ribera, in Agrigento, Sicily. I did some research, and I found her in the Ellis Island records as coming here in 1904. You see, there was a lot of economic strife in Sicily because of the earthquakes, and there were recessions and a lot of poverty there. And there was no economy, so they had to come to the United States to survive and really make money and live.

By that time, she had already four children that she came here with, with her husband, and landed right here in the East Village. They all came together on East Thirteenth Street. The earliest known address was 315 East Thirteenth Street, but the later address for my grandmother was 401 East Thirteenth Street

And my great-grandmother's maiden name, Giuseppa Colletti, could very possibly be related to a woman called Annie Colletti, who perished in the Triangle Shirt Waist Fire. So, I am currently working to make that connection with the family.

My great-grandmother was a housewife, and my grandmother…she was a superintendent of buildings in the neighborhood. Her husband had been sent to a mental institution. She had to make money for the family, but the family was broken up. Then she was working in the dancing business. She was a taxi dancer, along with my mother and my aunt, in Times Square and here on Fourteenth Street. They would do what they called "Dime a Dance." So customers would come in. They'd look at the girls—and they were all socializing and everything—and buy tickets to dance with the girls.

Joe Preston on East Eleventh Street in 2012. *Courtesy of Eric Ferrara.*

At the same time, my grandmother was cooking in one of the bars owned by a cousin here in the East Village. Well, she decided to buy the bar…on Twelfth Street and Second Avenue. She named it "Slugger Ann's Bar and Grill." The reason she got the moniker "Slugger" was in the dance hall when men would get fresh with her, she would have to hit them.

Back then you didn't worry about lawsuits or anything like that, so if somebody got fresh with you, it wasn't smacking, it was punching. I even have an article here. They did a whole interview with her holding up her mitts with boxing gloves. And she spoke about…not only did she punch out the men customers, but if one of her women co-workers got out of line, she did the same thing. She was a tough old broad, I'll tell you that. A tough young one, actually!

Josephine was my mother. She actually moved to this block, on Eleventh Street between Third and Fourth Avenues, in 1957. She had already had one child, my brother Robert, and he was born in 1951. I came along in 1959, and she brought me back from Bellevue, and I have lived on this block ever since.

My mother was working as a dancer. When I came along, she stayed home to take care of me. She couldn't do the dancing gig anymore. My father was not in the picture whatsoever; she was struggling. She was basically on assistance…public assistance…at the time. She couldn't work; my grandmother couldn't afford to support her. The rents in these apartments in 1957 were very expensive by comparison.

You know, when you're a kid, you just accept your surroundings. You don't say, "Gee, I wish I lived in the country. Gee, look at that rich kid over there, he's got a limousine and fancy clothes." Everybody was poor; you didn't know what you were missing.

Everybody was friendly. Everybody knew everybody. All the families were well connected. You were always eating in other people's houses or stopping by and saying hello. You could leave your door open all day long.

We played in the streets—we played stickball, football. In the street, we played handball, what we called Chinese handball, because it was against the building, you know what I mean? We played a game called Skellzies, right? Where we draw chalk all over the street and filled bottle caps with wax, you know?

We also played hide-and-seek in Webster Hall because the manager used to let us in! We'd bang on the door, "Could we come in and play?" and then lose each other for hours! I would go down into the basement, upstairs and all of this kinda thing. That was our playground.

Joe Preston's grandmother, Slugger Ann, circa 1955. *Courtesy of Joe Preston.*

Joe Preston and his friend Walter Hill playing on East Eleventh Street during the summer of 1968. *Courtesy of Joe Preston.*

My mother used to take me to Tompkins Square Park. She'd put me in the pool or something like that. We went for walks to Washington Square Park, also to Battery Park. It wasn't much of a park back then…they had the rail and the Staten Island Ferry. My mother would take the bus mostly 'cause she didn't like the trains. The Third Avenue El was torn down a couple of years before I was born.

My mother took care of the shopping and the laundry. There was an A&P right on the corner of Fourth Avenue and Eleventh Street during the '60s. We also had little bodegas around the corner, and she'd become a checker in Sloan's on Eighth Street between Broadway and University…on the north side of the street. So she was shopping there for groceries.

There was a laundromat on Tenth Street and First Avenue. It was terrible! Old washing machines and dryers, a thousand people in there, mostly women. During that time, men didn't do laundry, you know what I mean? And I remember the wringers because the washing machines didn't drain all the water out, so you put the clothes through the wringer. It's like dough coming out of two rollers. I'd go with my mother to help her, and it was so hot!

I went to P.S. 19 for grade school. After school, come home, do your homework. Got that out of the way, and then we'd run downstairs and play. We had roller skates—those old metal clunkers—skateboards, scooters. I hated carrying my bicycle up the stairs, but I was lucky. I had my own bike. We went all over the neighborhood, but there were some blocks you didn't go on. Tenth Street, between Second and First, was heavily controlled by drugs. You didn't go past First Avenue. The only reason I did was to go to Junior High School 60, which is on Eleventh Street and Avenue A. Or unless we were going to Mary Help of Christians on Twelfth Street and Avenue A.

We went to what you called "catechism." We'd get out of school at three o'clock in the afternoon, and then you went to Bible school after that. Plus being involved with Brother Frey…Reverend Frey…he'd constantly come to the neighborhood and take us places. He'd take us up to Rockefeller Center, out for ice cream or pizza or to play softball on the FDR drive and talk about the Bible a little and just do an outing. Because he knew a lot of the families couldn't afford to do that. In the summer, we'd go to Bible camp. His ministry sponsored it. You paid eight dollars a week to go, and some kids didn't even have the eight dollars.

The block was quite a mix during the 1960s, and I analyzed this, even as a child. We had Asian, we had African Americans, we had Latino—Latinos from different countries. Puerto Rican Latinos, Spanish Latinos, South American Latinos. And this was on this block and the next block. And around the corner, we had Italians, we had Polish, we had Ukrainian, you see? We had some Jewish. I happen to be half Jewish myself 'cause that's my father's side.

So, we had…every nationality was represented. And that's why until I got into my twenties, as naïve as this sounds, I didn't know that there was such strife going on in this country. I used to watch the news programs and tried to understand what was going on. And the turmoil of 1968, all the race riots and everything. I didn't believe that was true.

Tremendous sense of community—everybody knew each other. Everybody was friendly to one another, protective of one another. The families were stable. They were hardworking, lower-class families.

After six o'clock in this neighborhood, you could hear a pin drop because the manufacturing placers closed late afternoon. On Twelfth Street and Third Avenue, that whole building was a manufacturing place. All the hardworking people were home, having dinner, watching television. In the late summer nights, and stuff like that, you would find people sitting out on their steps, congregating and talking to one another. It was community.

What lacked back then might be the modern conveniences of the home today, but there was no shortage of people being friendly to one another. It was lovely and supportive. What it lacks today is that connection. Yeah, we might have a lot of fancy, expensive condos in this neighborhood, but I got people in this building who pass me on the steps and don't even say, "Boo." Don't say, "Hello." So, it's a different world, in some senses. I would change it—trade it off—for that '60s and '70s era in a second.

If people were short on food, everybody would ask each other if you had extra this, extra that. "You have eggs? You have milk?" This or that. "Oh, you don't have enough to eat? Come to my house, we made plenty." You know what I mean? And we all went in each other's homes, knock on the doors…there was no formal invitation, you just went by and said, "What are you doing?" You know what I mean? So that was pretty tight. In that sense was lovely.

I went to the High School of Art and Design. So I started getting part-time jobs after that. I was a graphic artist for eight years, and I decided to give that up and go into the antique business. I excelled in art; since I was in kindergarten, they saw a talent in me. I had friends of the family that were pushing me to go the art route, but I never did.

My cousin was in show business—Jackie Curtis, who started in the Warhol factory and who is my first cousin and godfather. A big Broadway producer and a lyricist and director is working on a new musical on Jackie's life—incorporating my family into it—which will open at LaMama this spring. And hopefully, if things go well, it might go to the Great White Way. So, we'll see. I'm just very, very proud of that...his legacy is also carrying on the family name and tradition.

I started realizing that living in a metropolitan area—or specifically the Lower East Side—gave me an advantage that I was aware of a lot more things maybe than Middle America was, just by being exposed to so many different cultures. We had Chinatown, we had Little Italy, we had Uptown. So I was exposed to all of these things, and I felt I had a little bit of an edge, you know?

In the late '60s, the landlord was warehousing these apartments by not renting them out. His plan was to eventually tear them down and build a high-rise. The Metropolitan Council of Housing got hold of what they were doing, and we formed a tenants committee. I was ten years old, but my mother took me to the meetings. We'd meet in the art galleries around the corner, on Third Avenue. The tenants decided they'd get people who were homeless, break the doors down and move them into the apartments. One night, I heard banging, and I was wide awake at three o'clock in the morning. The landlord was eventually able to evict them, but for five years after that, the tenants were just not moving. My family had been on the Lower East Side a hundred years, so my mother was not one to move. Finally, this compromise came up of moving into 114, and we did. We stuck together and held out...and we're living proof that these buildings were good and sound. And thirty-five years later...here I am.

Nilda Rivera

*Interviewed in June 2001 at Mrs. Rivera's apartment
on East Thirteenth Street*

We came from Puerto Rico in the early '50s, from Ponce. My father came first, and he was working in New Jersey. He started out as a dishwasher, and eventually he was the chef. My mother worked in all kinds of places. Factories...not sewing. It was more like making pocketbooks and things like that in Brooklyn. Her last job was a payroll secretary at the Board of Ed.

When I went to school, it was very mixed. There was still a lot of Jewish people, Puerto Rican kids that had recently arrived, Irish, Italian, even Maltese kids and African American kids.

In school, the assistant principal gave me this test to see how much English I spoke. I said one of the words I'd learned that I thought was English, but it wasn't. It was Yiddish...*meshugenah*. And she was Jewish, and she laughed. She thought that was the funniest thing. Then I was placed in a huge class with all these kids that had just come from Puerto Rico. I don't think the teacher spoke one word of Spanish.

I don't know how we learned, but we learned. We'd turn around and ask the other kids, "What did he say? *Que dijo?*" And the kid would tell you, and the teacher would yell at you, "No Spanish, only English! Five demerits for you."

And in those days, you got five demerits for chewing gum, for talking, for silly things like that. At the end of that year, we were promoted to another class where we were with everybody...in a regular English class with kids that were Irish, Jewish, Italian.

Nilda Rivera on East Thirteenth Street in 2012. *Courtesy of Eric Ferrara.*

I spoke Spanish at home. My mother and father eventually learned English. I wanted to be a part of the culture, and the only way I was going to get access to it was to speak English. Rock 'n' roll…black radio stations, jazz—I wanted to understand what they were saying.

At that time, rock and roll was not allowed to be played on the radio stations. It was considered immoral and decadent. I laugh about what some people say about hip-hop because they thought that rock and roll would be the death of this country.

I was living at 53 Norfolk Street between Broome and Grand. I lived in what they called Cherry Hill, which would be from Avenue D going up toward Grand Street. Historically, there was a hill there that had cherry trees. It was a walk-up building; we were on the third floor. The bathrooms were in the apartments, but the tub was in the kitchen.

I didn't go to clubs much. It was more like on weekends you went to the movies. There were lots more movies then. There were about nine theaters in that neighborhood. On Clinton Street itself there was two theaters. A big Loews that had first-run movies, then farther down they had a cheapie movie between Houston and Stanton. On Delancey they had the New Delancey that only played old Mexican movies. Then there was a Loews Canal on Canal Street. There was another theater on Grand Street that you could go in for twenty-five cents and see kiddie matinees—two movies and twenty-five cartoons on a Saturday.

On Friday nights, the community centers would have dances. It was like a community service to keep the kids from trouble. You just went from one center to the other to see who had the best dance.

I went to Catholic Church first, and that didn't last because the priests were kind of harsh. One of my cousins went to the Episcopal Church on Henry Street, St. Christopher's Chapel. And they had a great youth program, so I'd go there. My mother was horrified that I was going to an Episcopal Church. But they'd take us to the theater, the beach in the summer. And the priest was a really funny guy. He'd take us to a nice beach out there on Long Island where you'd have to pay. And he'd wear his white collar and talk his way out of it. "These are poor city children; I'm bringing them to the beach."

At that time, in the '50s, there was a lot of gangs. There was violence. There were kids stabbed. But I had nothing to do with that. I was more into other things—going to church, reading and listening to the radio.

We went shopping on Orchard Street. Things were cheap. You had outside bins. The owners would stand outside and hawk things. But generally, you didn't want to be known as having shopped in Orchard Street. So whenever you shopped in Orchard Street, you hoped your friends wouldn't see you. They'd be shopping in Orchard Street, too, but they'd tell you, "No, no, I was just walking there with my mother."

Food shopping? We went to the supermarket that used to be near Chinatown, on Market Street. My little brother and I used to go with the shopping cart, buy food and schlep it all the way back to Norfolk Street.

Not only that, there weren't that many laundries, so we'd take the laundry to Market Street, start washing it there. Do the shopping while the clothes were being washed, come back, bring the groceries, then go back and get the clothes. So we had to do four trips. When I think of it, that was really hard work. We did that on Saturdays or after school.

We had a dog named Brownie. He looked like a little wolf. He was a very independent dog, so he walked all over the place without a leash. Wherever you were going, he'd run out the door and go with you. He went shopping. He even went to church once.

You know that Norman Rockwell painting where the people are in church and the dog walks in? Well, I remember exactly. He walked right in. We were at St. Augustine's, an African American church that dates back to colonial times. It was Ash Wednesday. They were giving out ashes, and Brownie followed us, and he walked right up to the altar, sniffed and walked out. I was pretending that he wasn't ours.

A sense of community? Yes. Everybody knew each other, and it was a mixed community. There were a lot of elderly Jewish people and Jewish storekeepers. There was an iceman across the street. He sold ice, and he carried the ice to them on his back. In those days, it was totally different—you could leave the doors open.

On Delancey Street, you could go out in the morning, leave your door open and nothing would ever happen. Nothing was ever stolen. We had maybe one key that my mother used when we went away for the day. Other than that, the door was always kept open, and we just came in and out.

I grew up having all kinds of friends. Even when I didn't speak English, I used to walk home from school with some of the Jewish kids. Somehow we communicated, I don't know how. Growing up on the Lower East Side, I grew up with everybody. And I joke with people, and I tell them I'm a little Chinese, a little Jewish. I'm a little Puerto Rican, I'm a little black—and I believe that I am. I grew up enjoying the Jewish holidays.

On Chinese New Year, I'd go to Chinatown where I had a "Chinese grandfather." He really wasn't, but that's what I called him. He had a bar in

Chinatown, and he'd give us a red envelope with money in it. So I grew up with aspects of different cultures.

The Jewish neighbor next door—the first time I saw her, she had numbers on her arm, and it was blue. I must've been about thirteen. She told me about the concentration camps and how her husband had died there. And I asked her why she didn't have the numbers removed. And she said, "No." It was important to keep the numbers…to remember. She had short red hair…reddish blond. And she always kept her purse in the kitchen hanging from a hook. And sometimes she'd give us candy and matzohs. And then I'd go hang out with my black friends, have dinner at their house and eat their food.

I've lived mostly on the Lower East Side, but I've traveled a lot. I got to go to the Soviet Union when it was the Soviet Union, to study theater. I remember sitting there and thinking how exciting it was because it was always my dream to go there. And I was like—I come from a little place in Puerto Rico. Ponce is a big city, but I came from a little…like a little hollow by the river. And I thought, I'm the girl that was born there, and here I am in the Soviet Union. To me that was incredible. It was like being in the moon. It was amazing. So in many ways, I've had a rough life, but I've had a magical life, too.

ORLANDO ROSARIO

Interviewed in January 2001 at Orlando's apartment
on Thirteenth Street and Avenue C

My name's Orlando. I'm Puerto Rican. I was born in New York City. Actually [Puerto Ricans] that were born in New York City we're known as Nuyoricans. My parents are from Puerto Rico. My father was from Quebradilla, Puerto Rico, and my mother was from San Sebastian. They came in the late '40s to look for a better way of life because there was a lot of poverty in Puerto Rico. As soon as they got here, my mother, my aunt, they worked in clothing factories. My father also did factory work. He was a carpenter and a furniture finisher.

I was born on Fourth Street between B and C. We were up on the fourth floor in a five-story walk-up tenement. The color for me then was gray; everything was gray, black and white. I remember I was about five or six years old, going in between the legs of people and seeing my first dead person on the street. People taking pictures with the big flash bulbs and photographers photographing people.

I also liked to hang out on the fire escape in the summer, looking up at the sky and the stars. It was beautiful 'cause I lived next to the last floor. That was my own private space. I'd hang out for hours just looking up with my blanket.

I played in the streets near Fourth Street and FDR Drive. Some of the games we played when we was young…Kick the Can. It was like hide 'n' seek. And it was deadly serious. You count, and if you see somebody, he has to kick the can before you grab it and call his name. And sometimes you grab the can at the same time he was going to kick, and he kick you in the face. It got bloody.

And we played hot pizza and butter with a belt. The guy hides the belt. And he has to say hot, hot, warm, warm, hot. And if you find the belt, you have to run quick to a neutral zone so you won't get hit with the belt. It was wild.

One of the famous games was Scully. You played that with soda caps. And we used to find all kinds of ways to soup up the caps—put glass in it or weigh it down with clay. That way if they hit you, they can't move you.

And one of the other sports we had was kite flying. We built our own kites from scratch. We took tissue paper and bamboo sticks from those bamboo shades and glued the sticks to the paper. And you'd tie a big tail on the kite and put razor blades on the tip of the tail. I'm serious. Then there'd be guys on the other roof flying the same kites with razor blade tails. And the point of the game was to make your kite spin and cut the other guy's line. We used to do that for hours. We'd battle in the sky.

There used to be pigeon coops on the different roofs. Raymond…I remember him from when I was twelve years old. He flew a lot of pigeons back then.

And one of the games was to make your birds fly at the same time and try to get your birds to connect with some of the other guys'. This guy on Avenue A sold a lot of pigeons, all different types, different prices. It was a sport back then.

And remember the maroon bikes with the banana seats? My brother built me one from scratch. We found the parts all over the neighborhood. And skateboards. We'd get one of those wooden crates and a big two-by-four. You get a roller skate and break it in half. You put one wheel in front and one in the back. And you have a skateboard.

What are those things they're selling now for a hundred dollars. We used to build those. And we built go-carts, too.

And in the summer, we'd be playing with the fire pumps, hosing down with the cans. They were hard aluminum cans not like these cheap soda ones. We'd scrape them on the floor all day till the tops fell off, then we'd sit by the pump and spray the cars, the people.

We'd tell people, "Go ahead, we're not going to get you." And as soon as they'd go by, with their girl, their friend. Pssssssh. We'd spray everybody. Then we'd run away. We were so silly.

I used to go to P.S. 15 near the store where they made the matzohs…by Forsyth and Houston. And they used to give us matzohs. I loved those crackers, but there was a lot of tension in '65 because of Kennedy's assassination and Martin Luther King and the commotion with Malcolm X. So I think that's where a lot of animosity came from…between different groups.

The Jews used to have synagogues in the neighborhood; there was one on Fifth Street in back of the school, and there was another one on Fourth Street. I recall an incident where Hispanics and blacks were attacking Jews, running them out of the neighborhood.

There were some Jewish merchants in our area, right on Avenue C. But we didn't see too many of them after a while. But it was the '60s, man, and there was a lot of stuff going on. People were angry…about conditions. We felt like we was in poverty.

I remember I had to stand in line with my mother to get cheese, to get powdered milk and cans of peanut butter. The "Cheese Line," we'd call it. We used to make some mean grilled cheese. The cheese line was right there in the projects on Avenue C. But that helped a lot because there were a lot of times we would open the cabinets and all we had was like the peanut butter or the powdered milk. Somehow we managed to make ends meet and survive…and eat. It wasn't all that bad.

My mother was a good cook. We ate a lot of rice and beans, fried chicken…*pollo frito* and *pollo guisau*…stewed chicken cooked Spanish style.

On Fourth Street and Avenue C, there's a restaurant, Adelas, where my mother worked for years. She was a waitress, and she made a little money on the side collecting numbers. It's still there, and I go there when I want a nice home-cooked meal.

School? I didn't go much to school. When I got to about the fourth grade, I used to just skip class—go walk around the park, FDR Drive Park by the river. I love looking at the water and the seagulls. One time I got caught, and they brought me to my mother, and I got a whooping. But it never stopped me. School was boring. I felt it wasn't alive enough for me.

Tompkins Square Park—that was my favorite park. Mayor Lindsay had just built the swimming pool. They had the big band shell. They used to have bands that played…great bands. They used to play congas there all the time. They played timbales, and they'd really jam—conga jam. And there'd be like five, six, eight, congas going, and they'd be throwing down rhythms. You could hear 'em for blocks. You could hear congas on Fourth Street, and they'd be playing like on Eighth Street. And you'd hear the beat—boom, boom, boom. And it would be the summer; it's hot, the sun is bright. The sounds are coming out of the park, and you hear these beats—tah, tah, tah-tah, tah, tah-doom, tah-tah, doom, tah-tah, da, de, da, de, da, de-da, de, da, de, da, de.

There was always white people around; there was always an intermingling. There was blacks, Hispanics and whites. The only people I remember

Casa Adela on Avenue C in 2012. *Courtesy of Eric Ferrara.*

moving out was some of the Jews. The Chinese were in Chinatown, the Italians were in Little Italy, but this area was always rich like that, mixed. I had a white girlfriend or a black girlfriend; there was always mixing. It was never discouraged.

Early '70s platform shoes came out; the bell-bottom pants with the big fat cuffs. Everybody started hanging out. I only went to junior high school—that was it. All I wanted to do is party. Gangs…a lot of gangs back then. Most of my brothers and sisters were gang members. I was a wannabe gang member. I had dances at my mother's house—"sweat parties." The red light on, the record player playing, slow music, grinding music, grinding down to the ground. Dirty dancing was nothing compared to this stuff.

In the '70s, the neighborhood got pretty bad. Buildings got burned down. Businesses closed. Because gang members—to get high—were burglarizing from one end of the avenue to the other. They'd break in through the ceiling, through the walls. They'd steal Pampers, milk, cigarettes and beer. The beer would go to the clubhouse. We used burnt-out buildings…find an apartment…run extension cords through it, hook up some lights, hook it up into a clubhouse. We'd bring all the beer there, the cigarettes, and get high. The pampers were for the guys that had kids. Young fathers couldn't afford them.

It got to the point, a lot of the guys from the neighborhood, they were in jail much of their life. A lot of violence. A lot of people carrying guns. You could see twelve-year-olds take somebody's life like it was nothing. Murder somebody in broad daylight in front of everyone. Over a couple of bucks, some drugs, ten dollars.

Before, you just used to have fistfights. I had my first fistfight in Tompkins Square Park when I was about eleven. This guy busted my eye open, but you learn how to fight. You didn't shoot everybody. If you had a problem you'd go to the park, they'd make a circle around you, and they'd put the two kids to fight and punch it out. They don't do that no more. Guys just want to grab guns. Don't even get the guy they're looking for. Shoot kids, mothers and everything.

It was about that time I moved my mother over here to Twelfth Street. She was on Fifth Street, between B and C. The building was going abandoned. A gang took over…drugs…shootouts. So when housing offered her this apartment, I told her, "Let's go!"

And I'm still here. I have a good job. I can get out of this area if I want to. But I feel comfortable here. My neighbors are pretty close on this floor. We all know each other. They know my mother for a long time. We all been through our ups and downs. The projects still have that.

And I walk through Seventh Street and Avenue C…and Ninth Street. And it's not personal no more. In the '60s, people were outside the buildings. There was music playing out of the windows. There was kids playing in the street. It was alive!

ERNESTO ROSSI

Interviewed in April 2012 at Mr. Rossi's store,
E. Rossi & Company, in Little Italy

This location that we're at now…is 193 Grand Street. We were located seven years ago at 191 Grand Street, and our store was at that location for over seventy years. Some new real estate group bought it. They rented to a restaurant. But in the end, they were nice enough to work with us, to move us next door, so we're still here. And I have to thank them for that because this area is going crazy.

My grandfather started the business in 1910. I have a picture here of my uncle Eduardo Rossi and my aunt Concetta Rossi. This in the 1920s, and if you look here, you can see that these are pianola rolls, for the player piano, and these here are music sheets. My grandfather was a music publisher, music from Naples from the 1920s and '30s.

I was born around the corner on Mulberry Street, above the famous Angelo Restaurant, in 1950. We lived on the fifth floor and then we moved to the fourth floor. God, if we only had that apartment today. We had bathrooms in the house, but we didn't have a shower. We had a bathtub in the kitchen… so if somebody had to take a bath, everybody outta the kitchen!

Tell ya' the truth, growing up here, I loved it. And I don't think I would trade it for anything. We grew up really simple. As kids we played in the streets, we played ball—stickball, whiffle ball, Kick the Can. We played touch football in the street. Luckily I never got ran over by a car. But actually, we felt like the streets belonged to us. We did what, when, whenever we wanted to. And then sometimes, in case we got too carried away, there was always someone there to put us in our place and say, "Hey, listen! You better

Ernesto Rossi at his store on Grand Street in 2012. *Courtesy of Eric Ferrara.*

Concetta (left) and Eduardo Rossi (right) with a customer inside the 187 Grand Street store in 1925. *Courtesy of John Rossi.*

Eduardo Rossi (seated) outside his store at 187 Grand Street in 1925. *Courtesy of John Rossi.*

stop that! I'm gonna tell your father! I'm gonna tell your mother!" I had a lot of friends.

As a kid, I went to Most Precious Blood Church, which is 109 Mulberry. I had Holy Communion there. Then I went to P.S. 130, which is on Hester and Baxter Street. Then my mother got us into a parochial school, called Transfiguration, which is in the heart of Chinatown, 29 Mott Street. And when I went to Transfiguration, it probably was split, fifty of Italian American descent and fifty of Chinese descent.

After that, I went to Seward Park High school…right here on Grand and Essex. I only went to college six months at night, then I trained for the National Guard. And when I came back, I went to work for a bank downtown. That's where I met my wife. We got married. We moved to Brooklyn. And when my dad passed away, he was ninety-five. On his deathbed, he turned to me and said, "Please keep my father's name alive." And after my uncle retired, I've been working here in the store every day. I'm down here seven days a week.

I loved growing up in the store as a kid. Besides selling Italian music, we also put out the Billboard Top 40 list every week. And all the kids in the neighborhood—if it was a Beatle song just came out, or an Elvis song, and prior to that, Sinatra on the 78s—they used to right away come to the store.

My father loved music. There were so many musicians in the store. Playing the guitar, it was easy. In the summertime, we'd play on the stoop outside, and when it got too late, some of the older ladies would get peeved, start throwin' hot water at us. I don't know where the hot water came from—if it came from the sink or where the hell it came from—just to shut us up!

My grandfather lived up the block on Mulberry up on the fifth floor. He was partially paralyzed, and he used to come down once a day. He'd come down very slowly, and if the weather was nice, he'd come and sit in our store. I'd bring him food to eat. Dinner time, I ate with him. Then he'd give me money and say, "Come back for coffee." So I'd go to Roma pastry shop, buy a couple of pieces of cake, and he'd make coffee.

My mother, she spoke to me in Italian, in a Neapolitan dialect. My father spoke to me in English, but in the house the two of them spoke Italian, yeah. He spoke a fluent Neapolitan dialect, my father. Back when people used to come from Italy, walk in the store and ask him what part of Naples he came from.

Don't forget, the early part of the century they only spoke Italian down on Mulberry Street. Little Italy actually extended from Bleecker Street down past Worth Street to even beyond that to where the Smith Projects are now on Madison Street…like Broadway to Chrystie and Eldridge Street.

Elizabeth Street was mostly Sicilian. And you had a lot of Neapolitans on Mulberry Street, where they have the San Gennaro Feast. As a kid, everybody would come down. Whoever moved out of the neighborhood always came down to participate in the feast or have a booth. We had what they called the "Grease Pole." The last day of the Feast they'd put up this pole, a telephone pole, and fill it with axle grease. And we'd choose sides and try to climb it.

My mother stayed home and took care of the housework. She'd make me coffee—black espresso coffee, half with milk—then she'd pour it, even on my cereal. I guess she wanted to put enough caffeine in me so I'd get up and go to school. Then she'd make a fried egg, like a frittata, and she'd fill it with ricotta cheese. And for dinner she'd make pasta...but all different types of pasta—pasta with beans, with peas, escarole soup. Actually, the peasant food. When my uncles would come up, she'd cook for everybody.

All the shopping was done local. She'd go to Alleva's cheese to buy mozzarella, eggs, dairy products, parmesan. At that time, you had many Italian butchers here. Then there were a couple of Italian fruit and vegetable guys. One guy was named Rudy. I went to school with his son Vinnie.

And there were the Carusos, right on Mott Street. And they were the last ones left. So there's not even an Italian fruit and vegetable guy anymore. There was one guy on the corner, sold just bananas—"Joey the Banana Guy." He had a pushcart...now, they're all gone. And around the corner a store named Ernie's. You went in there and you had pasta, but not in boxes, loose; you had bins of all size pastas. And Di Palo's cold cuts were the best. In fact, Martin Scorcese says when he was kid growing up in Little Italy, his mother used to send him to Di Palo's.

Ferrara was next door; he had a pastry shop. And then there was Roma Pastry Shop. There was a store called Fontanelli's. We used to shop there for all our canned foods. There was no big store to shop in; you needed a roll of paper towel, you needed a roll of toilet paper, Yankee Doodles, whatever you needed, we all shopped in Fontanelli's.

And what else did we have? Oh, we had several pizzerias, naturally. Across the street from me now, there's a place called Florio's. It's a restaurant pizzeria. The original Florio's, that started I think in the early '60s. His son was a Yankee batboy, and when you went in there, you'd see all the Yankee paraphernalia. He made the greatest pizza. Really great, fantastic.

There was a bakery on Elizabeth Street, and they made Sicilian pizza, ten cents a slice. That was probably the late '50s, early '60s. Ten cents! And they were big! So if you had a buck, you were a king. And every block had a little grocery. You didn't go to a large store to buy anything; there was no like Pathmark and all this stuff.

There was a club on every block. You didn't have all these restaurants like you have now. And guys were in those clubs all night, playing cards, drinking and talking. It was a very safe area. If a woman or anyone walked up the block and yelled, someone would come to their aid immediately. If someone was walking up and down these streets and they looked suspicious, someone would come out of their club and say, "What are you doing here? Who are you looking for?" So the area actually policed itself. Everyone watched out for everyone.

Little Italy and Chinatown…we're neighbors. We respected them, and they respected us. I went to school in Transfiguration Church. The guy I went to school with, his name was Joseph Chan, and he was the first Chinese American police officer in New York, I believe. We also went to Seward Park High School together. And his father owns a…they make tofu…a tofu factory right in the heart of Chinatown, and we're great friends.

Growing up here, I look at Little Italy and Chinatown as being one. You walked south of Canal, you're in Chinatown. If you walked down Grand Street past the Bowery, down to Orchard and Ludlow, you're in the old Jewish section. As a kid, my mother used to bring me there to buy all my clothes—Orchard Street, Ludlow Street. And the store keeper would say, "Mama, come inside…Mama! I got some nice clothes for the kid! Come in!"

Walking down Orchard Street, walking by those big barrels of pickles. It was a nickel for the pickles. And then the guy selling knishes, fifteen cents a knish, a sweet potato.

If you walked west of Broadway, you'd walk into Greenwich Village. I had an aunt who lived on Christopher and Gay Street. Yeah, so you were in Greenwich Village. Wherever you walked, you walked into a different neighborhood. It was fantastic, right?

MYRON SURMACH

Interviewed in September 2001 at Mr. Surmach's
Ukrainian gift shop at 11 East Seventh Street

I am Myron Surmach. The infamous Myron Surmach of 11 East Seventh Street in New York City. I was born on Seventh Street in 1932...March 9. We used to live on Fourteenth Street. We moved around quite a bit. We moved around five times before I was nine years old. And then we settled out in Queens. My dad had purchased a bungalow in East Elmhurst prior to the construction of La Guardia Airfield, and we moved there.

And that was my beginning. From age nine to eighteen, we stayed out in Queens in East Elmhurst. Then I joined the navy, came back here in 1955. And my dad waved goodbye to me as he went to Saddle River, New Jersey, to a farm he had purchased to raise bees.

And he explained to me that beekeeping was a very sacred and noble pursuit because in the old world, in Ukraine, sugar was for the aristocrats. And every farmer could have his own beehive and surprise his family with the sweets they needed to bake. My parents came from Ukraine; born in Halychyna. It's in western Ukraine. I speak and read and write the language, having absorbed it with my years here.

My dad was a sheepherder, and at the age of fifteen, while tending sheep, he said, "You know, I could do something a little more than watch these sheep." So he applied for a visa to the United States.

When he got off the boat at Ellis Island, he was fifteen years old. Didn't know the language, didn't know the customs, didn't know anything. A real pioneer. And he went to work in a coal mine. He heard they needed strong backs and weak minds in the coal region of Pennsylvania. They put him

Myron Surmach at his shop on East Seventh Street, circa 1980. *Courtesy of Markian Surmach.*

underground to open up the doors between cars. It smelled, and it was dark. And there was water dripping. So he stayed there two weeks, and he says I can't take it. But he could read. People were amazed. So in the boardinghouse where he lived—at night, with a kerosene lamp—the men would sit in this boardinghouse parlor and talk to each other and smoke.

So my father says, "You want to hear something from a book?" It was like entertainment at home. There was no television, no radio, just their own talking to amuse them. So he started to read from a book, and they were delighted.

And they brought him a book. "Read this to me. Read this." And pretty soon, he said, "Why shouldn't I open up a business and have books that people can read?" And he went to New York City. Right on this block, there was a church across the street. And he said, I think I'll put my shop next to a church. Because people go by on Sunday, and they're sure to see something in the window that they want. And that was in 1918. He sold paperback books and newspapers.

When I came back to New York in the '50s, it was depressing. I tried to figure out what I was going to do for the rest of my life. My dad waved goodbye to me, and he went up to Saddle River, New Jersey. He said, "The store…It's yours. Do whatever you want with it." We owned the building, so the rent was cheap. And I started to bring in things like…I went to Romania and brought back embroidered blouses and was fairly successful with it. *Hair* was being presented on Broadway, and all the girls came in…then the Jefferson Airplane…then all these rock groups. Janis Joplin…they all wanted something different…and I brought it on.

The street. It's always been residential. The church was down the block—St. George's Ukrainian Catholic Church—I was baptized there, married there. They built a new church, and they moved it to the corner.

The architecture around here has changed. There used to be stoops where people would sit and talk into the night, and I'd sleep on the fire escape. I lived in this building. It was neighborly. Everybody knew each other since it wasn't a transient building. All the buildings were occupied by family groups. If you got along with the person on your floor, you'd trade recipes. I know my mother used to trade recipes with Mrs. Engalia across the hall. It was typical Hollywood. "Can I borrow a cup of sauce?"

At that time, I didn't regard it as anything interesting, but looking back—sitting on the fire escape—that was our balcony on the world. Looked down at the cars passing by. It was a community as much as it was a neighborhood.

My dad was like an impresario. He loved the arts. He also loved being a community leader, which he was. He would organize six buses to take widowed or lonely mothers on a day's jaunt into the country on Mother's Day. They would sing songs of the old country that they left. I was on the bus. They were all nice old ladies, old *babushka* ladies. They'd have potato bag races, one leg in each side of the potato bag. And he'd have them run.

They had a lot of fun. They also drank a little bit on the bus to remember the songs.

And then he ran balls at Webster Hall right here on Eleventh Street. Year after year after year. Twenty years in a row, Surmach's Radio Ball…because he had a radio program too.

He had a lot of stuff going. And he said, "Whoever meets at this Surmach Ball tonight and goes on to get engaged and married, I will pay for their honeymoon." And he did…up in the Catskills. He was full of ideas, and I admired him for that.

Now my kids admire me. But not for the same reasons, for totally different reasons. And I say, my God. Don't admire me. I've not done much. I've just maintained the business. And they think it's great.

Sundays, that was my day off. You go to church, and the priest knew it if I wasn't there. People look at you to do the right thing when you're a shopkeeper. If I didn't go to church, the priest would ask, "What, you sick?" Oh, he'd question me. I did my best.

On Sunday afternoons, I usually went to Washington Square Park with my son and daughter, carrying my son on my shoulders and pushing my daughter in a carriage. My wife would come with me. We'd go down to South Ferry, take the ferry across. Oh, we'd find ways of enjoying ourselves until it got dark.

Back in 1939, we lived on Tenth Street right across from Tompkins Square Park, in the middle of the block on the north side…in one of those town houses. The park back then.

There was a lot of horse traffic. There were horses drinking water out of the troughs at the side. There was the vegetable man yelling down and the women yelling from the windows. And there was the iceman. He would yell up. "Hey, ice! Hey, ice!" And he would walk up five flights of stairs for ten cents. Just to deliver a piece of ice to an icebox. And it was all par for the course.

By the '50s, most people had electricity. Some people didn't want to use electricity. That was an extra bill. Before that, there was just gas. Gaslight and gas cooking. Then electricity came in, and everything happened at once. Some people got electrified. No…no…I didn't mean that.

And then they didn't want to use the electricity. They were happy with the way it was. At night we go to sleep; in the daytime we read. They weren't interested in plugging this big monster into the wall and having it cool the food in there because the ice is fine, and the iceman is dependable. And it's cheap; ten cents every week.

How has living on the Lower East Side changed my life? I'm not surprised at anything anymore, having passed so many years here. The neighborhood was a community with maybe four distinct ethnic groups participating. St. Marks Place was the Polish block. The Electric Circus…that was the Polish National Home. And Seventh Street was a Ukrainian block. Second Avenue was Jewish.

And there was a smattering of Italians all around. But we all lived together. I guess everybody was happy to live here because of what was going on in the rest of the world…war and conflict. When I was joining the navy, I asked my father if I should do it. He said, "I don't think you'll regret it." This is the best country in the world. If you cooperate with this country, you'll benefit. So I did. And he was right.

In memoriam of Mr. Myron Surmach, who passed away in July 2003. His family continues to operate the store.

Rabbi Harold Swiss

Interviewed in December 2002 at a coffee shop on
Twenty-second Street and Third Avenue

I lived on the Lower East Side with my grandparents. My grandfather was crippled; he came from Russia...Kiev. We lived on Eldridge Street, which was a very narrow street. On Ludlow Street, there's the Romanian synagogue. About three years ago, I passed by it. I hadn't been there since I was a child. I walked in. I saw the rabbi. I introduced myself. I said, "I am Rabbi Harold Swiss of the Village Synagogue and when I was a child I sang here with Yossele Rosenblatt, the greatest cantor that ever lived." He said, "I want you to do me a favor. I want you to go to the ark and stand in the same place you stood when you were a child, and sing as though you remember your childhood. And sing what you sang then." I tell you, I wanted to fly away. I'm recapturing my youth in one second, singing from that same spot.

On Clinton Street, I used to like to walk there. One day, I found fifty dollars, and I spent all my money on Orchard Street. My grandmother didn't believe me. She followed me. I was a real conniver as a child.

I went to P.S. 20 on the corner of Rivington and Eldridge. I had a good friend, Frank Rizzo. He was a wonderful child, an artist. That school's no longer there. P.S. 20's now on Essex Street. The synagogue where I went as a child, right across the street from me, now it's a housing project. The stable next door to me is still a warehouse. The people I knew on Eldridge Street were wonderful. Whether you were Jewish, Catholic, Protestant, black—it doesn't matter.

The public baths were on Essex Street. There was nowhere to bathe in the apartment. We had a toilet in the hall, and that's it for the whole floor.

A Sunday morning in 1915 on Rivington at Orchard Street. *Courtesy of the Library of Congress.*

The washbasin was in your house. In my house we had a flatiron stove. The flatiron stove served us for a lot of purposes. When it became red hot, you could put stuff on the stove and cook it; the sink only had cold water. You had to heat the water. And the icebox, you had to put ice in it.

I was really a conniver. A woman used to come to me and say, "Could you make me a phone call, please? I have to call my son-in-law." She gave me a nickel. I took the nickel and put it in my pocket. Then I took out a penny. And I put the penny underneath the trolley car, so when it went over the penny, it became the size of a nickel. You understand? I made the phone call. I made four cents profit.

My grandfather was a wonderful influence in my life, morally and spiritually. I taught him English as a child. He felt very uncomfortable making a cross because a cross meant to him Christianity. He had to make a cross. It bothered him. So I had to teach him how to write his name: Mr. Abraham Finkelstein. He did that while I was sleeping. When I was little, I spoke Yiddish. I was a bright child. I had a tremendous interest in English. I learned it on my own. I also learned how to speak properly.

141

Eldridge Street was cobbled; you always saw the horses coming back and forth. Once in a while, you saw an old car. The horses used to go past our window. And my grandfather saw them disemboweling, so one day he said to me, "I want you to go pick up the making of the horse." And I said, "Could I mix it with the fertilizer?" He had a box outside his window where he grew corn and lima beans every year. So I went down to pick that up, and somebody from the top floor cried out, "Hey, kid, how much a pound?"

I used to hang around Houston Street, which is a block away from Stanton Street toward First, Second and Third Avenues, and on Houston Street there were a lot of knish stores. I got a job in a knish store selling knishes. I didn't last very long because I was a rough kid. I stole. Used to go around with that can…Jewish National Fund can…I went from place to place. And at the end of the day, when people contributed, I went back home. I took a knife, and I took out all the dollar bills and the big coins. I stole it.

The living? I have nothing to complain about. I didn't have to live with many people. I didn't have to live with anybody but my grandparents. But what happened then with most people who came over from the other side, they used to bunch up in one apartment. They'd be five, six people in one apartment. Maybe more sometimes. They'd sleep on the floor.

When you walk on Eldridge Street, toward 172 Eldridge Street, you will see my name is inscribed right on the cement. The last time I was there, it was still there. If you look north, you can see the Chrysler Building, a good part of it. I was watching it as it was being built.

When I was a child and it was wintertime, I was always happy to see that everybody had a big can. And they threw coal in it, and they made little fires all along Orchard Street. They were all peddlers with pushcarts selling combs and shaving and every kind of junk.

We had electric light; we didn't have gaslight. And every year about the same time, the lights were shut off—at least for about ten minutes—for the birthday of Thomas Edison, to commemorate his life and the fact that he gave us electricity. They don't do that any more. Now we take electricity for granted, but then it was such a nice thing to have electric. We had an electric fan; it went back and forth, alternating.

On Delancey Street, they had a cafeteria…Delancey near Clinton. I had forty cents in my pocket. Forty cents isn't too bad, but you couldn't eat a full meal, and I wanted a good meal. I went into the cafeteria, and I ordered myself a very good meal. It was about two dollars. Now as I walked in, I heard some Communists arguing with each other. I ordered my food and took a ticket. My ticket was two dollars and ten cents—but how am I

Celebrating the Jewish New Year, 1910. *Courtesy of the Library of Congress.*

going to pay it? Boy, I was so clever. I walked over to the Communists that were still arguing. And they had their tickets on the table, so I took the one with about twenty cents on it. I put my ticket back, and I walked out like a gentleman.

How do you survive that kind of environment if you don't steal? I used to steal fruit from the fruit stand, and then I found out the poor man was not making much of a living and I stopped doing it. When I went to Kittelstein's Delicatessen Store on Delancey Street, and I had ten cents in my pocket, I was able to get two hot dogs…with sauerkraut, mustard…for ten cents.

Rivington Street was a very fascinating street. There were stores there that sold all kinds of fruit, nuts. The wine store…Shapiro's. There's another thing on Rivington: as you walk up Eldridge Street toward Rivington, there was a big synagogue. It's still there. There was another synagogue on Allen Street and Eldridge.

One time in front of the Romanian synagogue, there was a bunch of anti-Semites who came to throw rocks at the congregants. They said, "You killed Jesus. You killed Jesus." So I said to them, "Do you realize Jesus was Jewish?"

"Who told you that? Jesus was never Jewish! Jesus was Christian! What are you talking about?" So they got angry with me, and they started throwing a rock at me. I took their hand, and I took their rock, and I held it just like that and they ran away.

The synagogue I used to go to was right across the street from me on Eldridge Street. It was where I was bar mitzvahed. I knew everybody there. In 1950, I did something that's extraordinary. I found a way to go into the synagogue and look around. I saw newspapers from 1917 to the time of 1950. I saw the gasoline cans where everybody warmed their hands when they came in from the outside in the wintertime. I saw the people. I saw the women sitting upstairs. (I never understood that, by the way. Could never convince me of that.) A month later, I came back. I wanted to do it again. But then it was a Greek church.

Growing up on the Lower East Side had the most positive influence on my life. In the midst of the poverty, I was learning, from older people, much older than me…in their eighties. And I learned so much from them. I used to walk with my hand behind my back like these old religious people. But I always was able to reach a smile.

In memoriam of Rabbi Harold Swiss, who passed away before this story was published.

Raymond Valentine

Interviewed in June 2001 at Tompkins Square Park

My name is Raymond Valentine, and I was born in Lincoln Hospital in the Bronx. My father and mother were born in Puerto Rico. My mother came to this country when she was thirty-six; she raised all eight of us by herself, so it was kind of rough for her. We lived on 241 East Seventh Street for fifteen years. It was a six-story walk-up. We had five rooms. I went to school on Ninth Street, where Charas is now. That was a school then. [Charas El Bohio was a community cultural center in the former P.S. 64 until it was sold to a developer in the late 1990s.] Then I went to P.S. 3 on Third Street between Avenue D and C.

I played hooky almost every day. I just wanted to be on the roof with the birds. So what happened was the truant officer caught up to us, and I went to reform school for two years. That's where I learned to read and write. I learned English. At home, my mother talked to me in Spanish. But she learned English on her own, hanging around with her friends and at the jobs she had taking care of elderly people.

Seventh Street was different than it is now. There was a lot of people playing stickball, people going to dances, going to gigs. They used to pay one dollar for the people to go to the house and have a party there. They had records. They used to dance until dawn. I went to Sloan Center for the kids that had no place to go. It was on 630 East Sixth Street between B and C. You play pool there; you dance. You have arts and music. Get to meet friends. Keep out of the street. I went there six days a week.

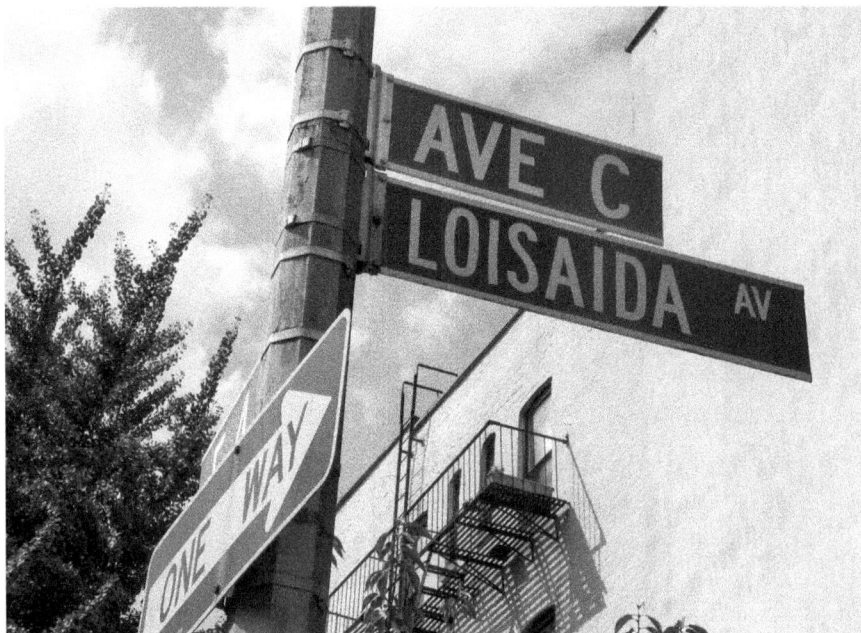

The term *Loisaida* was coined by the Nuyorican community of the 1970s. *Courtesy of Eric Ferrara.*

Tompkins Square Park is different than it was; it got renovated. Before they used to have Jewish, Ukrainian, Polish all mixing together, learning how to get along and understand each other because this neighborhood was for people to survive and to grow. Now the white people are taking over. Because they have more money.

In the past, there be a lot of gangs—the Viceroys, Untouchables, the Dragons, the Purple Gang, the Girls Gang. Most of the gangs used to fight, but they were like social gangs; they wasn't troublemakers. No, I never was in a gang. My only gang was being on the roof with my birds.

When I was a little kid, I was flying a kite one day, and I saw something in the yard that it couldn't fly. So I climbed down the fire escape, and I saw it was a bird. I took him home and bought him a girlfriend so he wouldn't be lonely. I found her at the pet shop. I kept him in the house. My mother didn't mind at first, but then the housing sent her a letter that she couldn't have no pets in the house, so she killed my birds. She put them in the soup pot. She did. I ain't talk to her for three months. I was about eight years old. Those were my first pets. I was really hurt.

I started to find more birds, but I never brought them home no more. I took care of them with my friend on the roof. I had about four hundred birds. We had the birdhouse on Stanton Street…Stanton and Attorney. His mother was a super over there; she let him take care of the birds on the roof. I was about sixteen. That's all I was interested in…being with the birds.

We bought them in the pet shop; those are domestic. Those are not the kind you see in the street. Those kind of birds…the only life they know is being on the roof and getting taken care of and making coo. See those kind of birds, if you have a house for them, they came back. They're not used to coming back in the street 'cause those are not trained birds. Not being with them is like a part of me is missing.

How you communicate with the birds…you whistle. And then they know it's time to eat; they come to eat out of your hand. They know when you open the door, it's time to go inside. If you know how to train 'em, they know how to find water. They know when it's time to sleep. They know when it's time to go outside. They know all those things. You just gotta have patience. I learned everything on my own.

Working with the birds, that's talent. You've got to memorize. And know them by markings. Every time my birds used to fly, I knew them by markings. I could tell which ones were not mine in the flock. I can tell you which ones are still out there and what colors.

Being with birds is the best thing to teach a kid; to raise up the right way. Growing up about nature. Teach you how to take responsibilities, not have your mind in dirt, being in the street using drugs.

When I was young, I had a fantasy. I always wanted to go to the army, be a war hero, become something of myself. But since I had this accident in my leg, they disqualified me. I never went back to school 'cause all I wanted to do is be with the birds. It's what God put me on this world for. It's my purpose.

STEVEN "PEPE" ZWARYCZUK

*Interviewed in October 2004 at McSorley's
Old Ale House on East Seventh Street, which Pepe has
managed for close to forty years*

My real name is Steven Zwaryczuk, but everyone calls me Pepe. I grew up in this neighborhood, and I played Little League Hard Ball with the Puerto Ricans on the FDR Drive. It was easier for them to call me "Pepe" than Zwaryczuk. That's my stage name.

No. I don't do theater…only here. The whole world's a stage…isn't it? You can quote me on that. Both my parents came from the Ukraine…from little villages on the western side of the Ukraine. They emigrated as "DPs" after the war…World War II; they were given a choice: either to come this way by the Americans or go back to Big Joe Stalin, who made Hitler look like an altar boy. They chose America. They came here. They landed in New York in December 1950. They were sponsored by farmers in Maryland and were supposed to be strawberry pickers. The church intervened; they sponsored them here instead.

Most of the people that migrated here had low-paying, low-level jobs, but they managed. They came in droves. Yeah…we were lucky; there were several families already here. There was a parish established…St. George…And the individual families took in my parents. At that time, there was just the two boys…my older brother Walter and four years younger…John. I and my twin brother, William, were born here in '55; by that time, we had our own apartment, and my mom had a super's job on Sixth Street between Second and Third Avenue…206 East Sixth.

It was great…millions of kids…millions of people…very diverse. In the building…for the most part we had a lot of Ukrainians…first wave.

They came here after the Revolution in the Soviet Union. But there were a lot of mixed families—some Spanish, some Chinese.

Diverse as this neighborhood was and still is…it's still very diverse. It makes us less critical of outsiders per se, because they were insiders here. We've always had a great mixture…a very great mixture of people here.

The street was our baseball arena, and for the most part every other sport kids in America played, except we didn't have fields. We used the streets; we punched ball, we played stickball, we played hardball, we played off the wall, we played tennis…makeshift tennis…makeshift basketball—you name it.

Everybody associated themselves with their particular block; all the Sixth Streeters played against the Seventh Streeters, the Seventh Streeters played against the Eighth Streeters. The archrival was always the Fourth Streeters because there was a bunch of Italian kids there who were good. Yeah.

Steven "Pepe" Zwaryczuk at McSorley's on East Seventh Street in 2012. *Courtesy of Eric Ferrara.*

Pepe outside McSorley's Ale House in 2012. *Courtesy of Eric Ferrara.*

When we got home from school, my mom was still home; she'd tend to us. My father would be sleeping because he got up early—he got up at two. He was at work at three in the morning, and he was home by around noontime. Most of his work was interior stuff that had to be done prior to the office workers coming in, then he had a couple of hours of outside work as well…washing windows. And shortly afterward, he'd be woken up, and she'd have to catch a bus to her building. Twelve o'clock at night and Dad would bathe us, feed us dinner. She'd cook it, and he'd eventually serve it to us…eventually. And he'd have to be in bed early because he'd be getting up at two o'clock and one of the older brothers would take care of us.

I went to a school directly across the street from where I lived, from kindergarten up until the end of high school. It was St. George…Ukrainian Catholic School. We all spoke American…English…what have you, but it was mandatory when you went to St. George to brush up on your Ukrainian. My parents…they spoke to us ONLY in Ukrainian. I learned

English just by living. I took English classes all the way through grammar school…high school. But we were lucky; we learned Ukrainian as well…grammatically.

Because our parents were people who came from a little town, they taught us the slang Ukrainian, and we learned the proper Ukrainian in school. You'd come home and you'd have a conversation with them, and you'd give them words and they wouldn't know what you were talking about. So we Americanized a lot of things. We called it half *navpil*…half and half; *navpil* is "half" in Ukranian.

It was difficult to have family get-togethers because one parent would be going and one parent would be sleeping. But for the most part, on Saturday, there was always something going on. If it wasn't a christening, it was a wedding. If it wasn't a wedding, it was some sort of community affair. We had so many Ukrainian organizations here that we all attended. There were several scout organizations. There was the Ukrainian Soccer Club that my older brothers belonged to, and there was always something going on in school. If it wasn't a bazaar, it was a bake sale. It was…something. Never ending.

Church? Going to this school here…St. George. During the school year, it was mandatory to go to church every day. Before we went to class, we went to church. From first grade through eighth grade, we went to Mass every morning. Yeah…Sundays we all went to church together as a family. Nobody was working.

There were a lot of movie theaters around here. We had the St. Marks movie theater; we had the Loews Commodore on Sixth Street and Second Avenue that became…later…the famous Fillmore East. That was a very popular movie theater for us. The St. Marks theater was smaller; it no longer exists. The Loews Commodore and the Fillmore East are gone now, too. That was turned recently into luxury apartments.

I recall after going to the theater my mom would take us to one of the Jewish delis on Second Avenue. All you got now is the Second Avenue Deli on Tenth Street. I remember at least a half a dozen different ones. We never even went to Tenth Street because that was too far.

There was one right around the corner here between Seventh and Eighth Street that was my idea of what a Jewish deli was. My favorite treat? It was always a hot dog with mustard and sauerkraut, French fries…plain and simple. Dr. Brown cherry soda.

I can recall going out to Coney Island. I don't recall any fond memories. All I remember is the straw seats on the train. And the straw coming up through my shorts and biting my ass. Because the train would be stopped there, and it would wait…because that was the last stop on the line. You'd wait and you'd wait and you'd wait, and there'd be no air conditioning, and the doors would be open. It'd be steaming hot. You're coming home. You're tired. You've got sand in your belly button. You've got sand everywhere, and you've got this long ride back into Manhattan. But sure, we took plenty of trips out there. I remember going to Orchard Beach, too, but I don't recall the place…just the name.

I remember parakeets and birds all over the neighborhood; everybody had a parakeet because Hartz Mountain was a manufacturer over here on Fourth Avenue just north of Fourth Street. They make pet food, canary food. I think they purposely let these birds out so people would catch 'em because then they'd have to feed 'em.

Shopping…for the most part…ethnic stores. Right now we just have one Ukrainian butcher over here on Second Avenue…between Eighth and Ninth Street, called Julian Baczynsky East Village Meat Market.

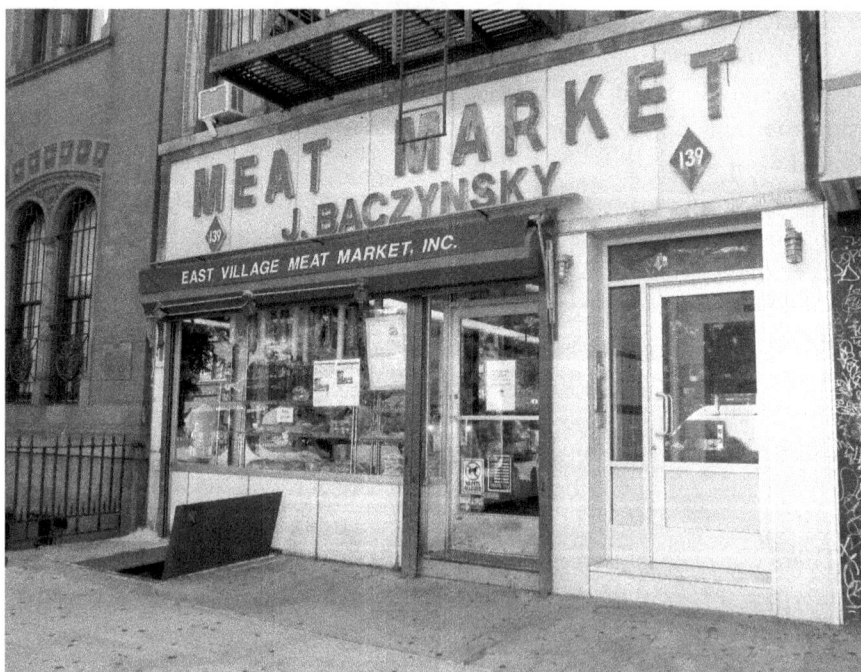

Baczynsky's of Second Avenue, the last Ukrainian butcher in the neighborhood. *Courtesy of Nina Howes.*

We used to always go to a place on Sixth Street and Avenue C. Two brothers owned the butcher store. But he got burnt out of there. Alphabet City was a bad neighborhood back in the '60s. He'd come to work, and the place would be burglarized. Those were tough times. Eventually, he came to work one day, and the business was up in smoke…literally…the smokehouse was up in smoke. Then my mother started shopping at another place here on Second Avenue called Brody, which they sold in the '80s. They were all getting older. And now everybody visits Julian Baczynsky.

Don't forget every street had a Ukrainian bodega. There was one here on Seventh Street before you got to Second Avenue. There was one on Sixth Street just past this old plumbing supply place, which is now an import/export Indian business. And there was one on every street. If you needed something fast, you could pick up milk here, bread there. You could pick up just about anything.

First Avenue was where the shopping was done for the most part—on the corner of Tenth Street and First Avenue. We went into that building quite often as kids. And inside there was a bunch of stalls, where you could buy pickles, where you could buy…not unlike the Essex Market. It was always dark, it was always dingy, it was always stinky. And then that was eventually taken over by the Department of Sanitation. And they used to store their equipment in that building…then *Bing!* That disappeared. And the theater was there.

We used to have a hotel right around the corner here…right on Sixth Street and Third Avenue. It's an empty lot right now…very sad. We met a lot of transient people. We didn't think of them as down and out, but for the most part they were. They were living in one room; sometimes there were families in one room. And the next thing I know, there's a court order and the place is sealed off and all those families are gone.

And there was a little store… a teeny-weeny restaurant underneath the place called Pops. They used to serve breakfast and lunch only. They had to leave their business as well. Yup. Them's the breaks. There used to be a slew of SRO hotels on every block on the Bowery. Slowly but surely they're disappearing.

Then you got this immediate neighborhood. There's Cooper Union. There's a building called the Bible House that no longer exists. They used to publish Bibles in there. Now it's the School of Engineering. The Tompkins Market no longer exists. This is before they raised the roof on it and made it an armory; there used to be a regiment that drilled on the roof. Yup! Before they moved the armory somewhere else. They tore that building down,

The new Freedom Tower rising behind the tenements of Henry Street in 2012. *Courtesy of Eric Ferrara.*

and they built this building here…and that's coming down now. And that's going to be classrooms for Cooper Union. [The new Cooper Union building opened in 2009.]

There's a church right on the corner of Seventh Street and Third Avenue. It used to be a bank. And now it's a Ukrainian Baptist Church. And then we got McSorley's. And Cooper Union Park. And pretty soon this whole area here is going to be one big park. They're going to eliminate the street. So it's stuff like that. Gets me excited. Change.

About the Authors

Eric Ferrara is a fourth-generation native New Yorker whose family has lived in Little Italy since the nineteenth century. He is founder and director of the Lower East Side History Project, founder of the Museum of the American Gangster in New York City and a consultant on several television and movie projects worldwide.

Nina Howes is a nurse, political activist and writer who was born and raised in New York City. Her stories have been published by Kaplan Publishing and the University of Iowa Press. Her plays have been presented off-off Broadway.

www.ingramcontent.com/pod-product-compliance
Lightning Source LLC
Chambersburg PA
CBHW070354100426
42812CB00005B/1507